How to Use, Adapt, and Design Sewing Patterns

Lee Hollahan

A QUARTO BOOK

First edition for the United States, its territories and
dependencies, and Canada published in 2010 by
Barron's Educational Series, Inc.

All inquiries should be addressed to:
Barron's Educational Series, Inc.
250 Wireless Boulevard
Hauppauge, NY 11788
www.barronseduc.com

ISBN-13: 978-0-7641-4425-7
ISBN-10: 0-7641-4425-1

Library of Congress Control Number: 2009938892

QUAR.USP

Conceived, designed, and produced by:
Quarto Publishing plc
The Old Brewery
6 Blundell Street
London N7 9BH

Senior editor: Lindsay Kaubi
Additional text: Sandra Wilson
Copy editor: Liz Dalby
Art editor and designer: Susi Martin
Art director: Caroline Guest
Design assistant: Saffron Stocker
Photographer: Philip Wilkins
Illustrator: Sha Tahmasebi, Chris Taylor, Katie Buglass
Picture researcher: Sarah Bell
Creative director: Moira Clinch
Publisher: Paul Carslake

Color separation in Singapore by PICA Digital Pte Ltd
Printed in Singapore by Star Standard Industries (PTE) Ltd

10 9 8 7 6 5 4

How to Use, Adapt, and Design Sewing Patterns

Contents

About this book

Making your own clothes allows you to get the perfect fit, and once you have perfected the fit, you can begin to add details of your own design. This book guides you through the process of using and adapting commercial sewing patterns to suit your body, and then moves on to explain how to create your own patterns using the pattern blocks provided in chapter 5.

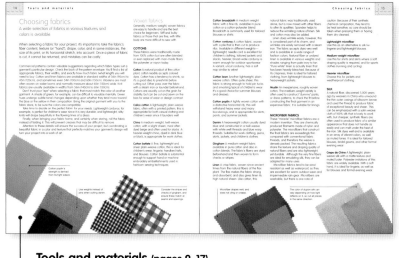

Tools and materials (pages 9–17)
Here you'll find a useful guide to the essential pattern cutter's tools and materials and the different types of thread available. There is also a directory of fabric types, with comprehensive information on fabric qualities and uses.

Use

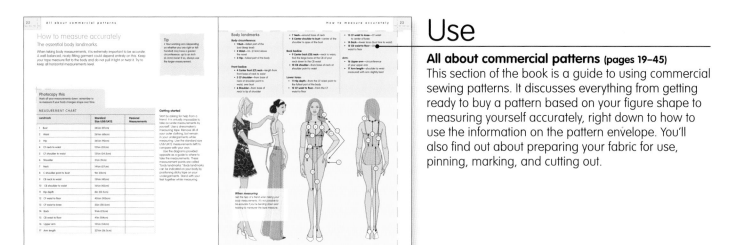

All about commercial patterns (pages 19–45)
This section of the book is a guide to using commercial sewing patterns. It discusses everything from getting ready to buy a pattern based on your figure shape to measuring yourself accurately, right down to how to use the information on the pattern envelope. You'll also find out about preparing your fabric for use, pinning, marking, and cutting out.

Adapt

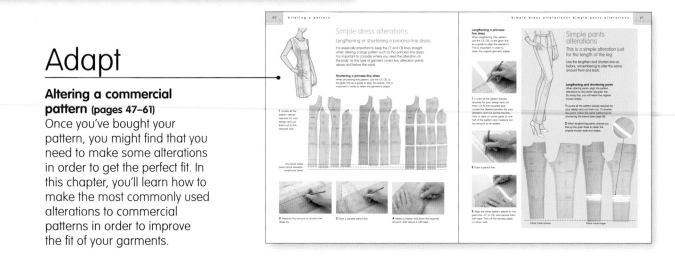

Altering a commercial pattern (pages 47–61)
Once you've bought your pattern, you might find that you need to make some alterations in order to get the perfect fit. In this chapter, you'll learn how to make the most commonly used alterations to commercial patterns in order to improve the fit of your garments.

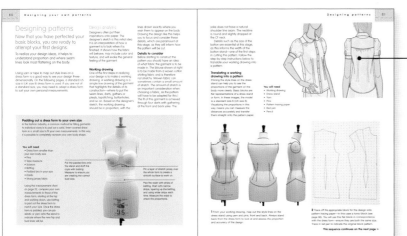

Design

Designing your own patterns (pages 63–109)

In order to design your own clothes, you need to create basic pattern blocks for all the components that make up a garment. In this chapter, you'll learn not only how to create these basic components using the pattern blocks provided with the book, but also how to manipulate them to different designs and styles that suit you. Find out about toiling your designs as an essential part of the making process, and how to transfer your two-dimensional design ideas into the three-dimensional reality of your own unique garments.

The pattern blocks
(pages 111–125)

In this section you'll find basic pattern blocks for a skirt, bodice, and sleeves in U.S. sizes 6–18 (U.K. 8–20). Scale the blocks up using the grid to make your own personalized pattern blocks. Tailor them to fit your figure and use what you learned in the previous chapter to design your own patterns.

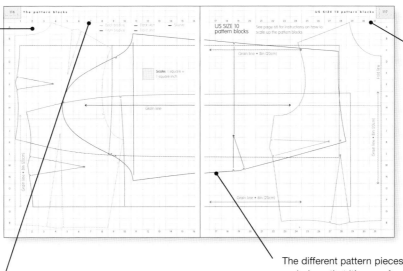

The blocks are laid out on a grid with squares that represent 1in (2.5cm), so that you can easily transfer the lines of the pattern pieces to pattern tracing paper.

The numbered grid helps you to keep track of where you are when transferring your design to pattern paper.

The different pattern pieces are color coded, so that it's easy for you to scale up the specific piece you need.

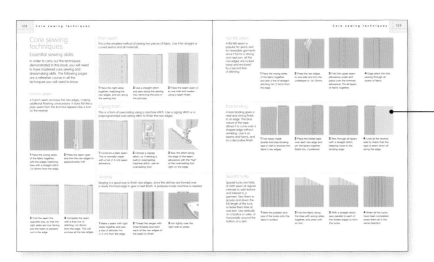

Core sewing techniques
(pages 127–139)

This refresher course on core sewing techniques serves as a useful guide for beginners or as a handy reminder for those already experienced in making their own clothes.

Tools and materials

In this chapter, you'll find all the information you need on the tools and materials essential for sewing and dressmaking. There is a guide to useful equipment and a full discussion on how to select the right fabric for your project.

Essential equipment

To get the desired quality of finish in your sewing projects, it's important to have the right equipment.

Over the next few pages, you'll find a guide to the essential tools for dressmaking and for designing and adjusting patterns. A guide to the different types of fabric can be found on pages 14–17.

Dressmaker's fabric shears

The long, straight, sharp blades of these shears give a smooth cut and are ideal for cutting fabric quickly. Often the handles are at an angle to the blades, so the blades can sit parallel to the cutting surface, ensuring the fabric remains flat. They have molded handles, with a smaller hole for the thumb and a larger one for the fingers, and can be right- or left-handed. They should be used only on fabric.

Serrated scissors

The fine, serrated edges of these blades hold delicate, lightweight, or soft fabric in place. They are ideal for fine fabrics, such as silk or satins.

Paper scissors

It's essential to keep a pair of scissors just for paper. Using fabric shears for cutting paper patterns will cause the blades to become blunt. Paper scissors do not need sharp points, but they must be able to cut paper cleanly.

Pinking shears

The blades of these shears have notched teeth that leave a definite zigzag edge on the cut fabric. This provides the "pinked" cut that neatens the raw edges on seams and makes the fabric less likely to ravel.

Needlework/embroidery scissors

Small and with short blades and sharp points, these scissors give greater control in intricate areas and are ideal for snipping notches, clipping curves, or trimming seam allowances.

Pattern tracing wheel

Used with dressmaker's carbon paper (also known as dressmaker's tracing paper), this tool transfers the line markings to both sides of the fabric at once. The method is not suited for heavy or textured fabric, on which the marks would be hard to see.

Needles

A selection of hand needles, in different sizes, is essential for hand sewing and for taking thread ends to the back of your work after machine stitching. For general machine sewing, universal (multipurpose) machine needles are available in different sizes to suit different fabrics and threads. For special purposes, such as sewing silk or doing decorative stitching, use specialist needles. Replace all needles regularly—blunt ones can snag fabric.

Wash-away marker pens

These can be used to transfer pattern marks to fabric. The ink from wash-away marker pens can be sponged or washed away afterward, but check that this does not damage the fabric.

Dressmaking pins

These general-purpose pins are used to hold pieces of fabric together before sewing. They are suitable for medium-weight fabrics. They are especially useful for working on paper patterns and when pattern drafting.

Tailor's chalk

Tailor's chalk is a traditional material used for marking cloth and can be easily brushed away when finished. It comes in triangular pieces, rollers, and pencils of various colors. Keep the edges or points sharp, mark on the wrong side of the fabric, and use a color that shows up well against the fabric you are using.

Fadeaway marker pens

Also known as evaporating or air-soluble pens, these are an alternative to tailor's chalk and wash-away markers. The ink fades in 48 hours, but test on a scrap of your chosen fabric first.

Pattern awl

This handy little tool allows you to hold and manipulate fabric when it would otherwise be too awkward for your fingers, for example, when guiding a gathered edge under the presser foot of a machine.

Tape measure

Choose a good-quality tape measure that will neither ravel nor stretch. It should be at least 60 in. (150 cm) long, with measurements marked accurately from the very start of the tape.

Pin cushion

It is a good idea to keep your hand needles and pins safely organized in a pin cushion, so that they are both out of harm's way and readily available when you need them.

Plain cotton fabric (1)

Inexpensive unbleached muslin, sheeting, or other plain cotton fabric is used for making toiles—test versions of a garment made to check the pattern (see pages 68–71).

Sewing machine needles

Multipurpose machine needles are suitable for regular machine sewing. These are available in sizes to suit the fabric and thread being stitched. American sizes range from 9–20 and European sizes from 60–120. Needle packets are usually numbered with the relevant size. The larger the number, the larger and stronger the needle.

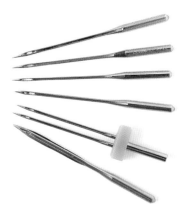

Dressmaker's tracing paper (2)

Used with a tracing wheel to mark fabric by transferring dots of color onto its surface (see page 44).

Dressmaker's pattern paper (3)

Marked with a grid to help you to create and adapt patterns, this can be bought ready-made or you can make your own.

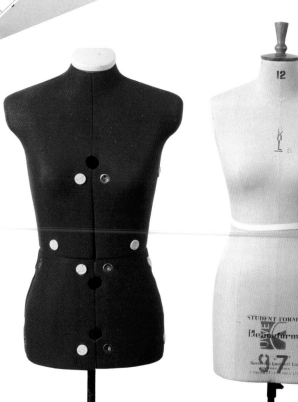

Dressmaking curves/Skirt curves

These templates, made of plastic, wood or metal and available in a variety of shapes, act as guides when drawing curves on a paper pattern, for example to shape hips on pants and skirts (see above and right). A 2 x 12in. (5 x 30cm) clear curve, with a ¼in (0.5cm) grid, like the one above, is especially useful.

Dress forms

These allow you to try out toiles (see pages 68–71) and to adjust garments for a better fit before final sewing. Adjustable dress forms are ideal models to start with. The dimensions can be easily adjusted to match your own or a friend's measurements. Solid, linen-covered dress forms are the fashion-industry standard. The clear seam lines help to achieve accurate pattern cutting, but they are only available in standard dress sizes and aren't adjustable (see "Padding out the dress form to your own size," page 80).

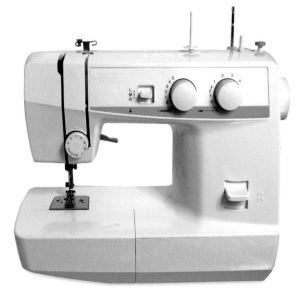

Sewing machine
A sewing machine is essential for anyone wanting to sew strong seams and give garments a tidy, professional finish. Machines work by interlocking an upper and a lower thread to stitch fabric layers together. The tension and the length of the stitches can be adjusted to suit the fabric. Modern machines offer a selection of different stitches for different tasks.

Iron and ironing board
An iron and ironing board are essential for ironing fabrics, and are also useful for smoothing out pattern pieces. Also useful is a tailor's ham; used for pressing curved areas of clothing, such as cuffs, waistlines, and collars.

Thread

The choice of thread will depend on whether it is for hand stitching or machine sewing. Choose a good quality thread in a fiber similar to the fabric being used, i.e., cotton thread for cotton; polyester for synthetic cloth, etc. Choose colors similar to that of the fabric so it blends in, or select a contrasting thread for decorative finishes. A good quality thread is essential when sewing.

General-purpose
Spun from polyester or mercerized cotton, or with a cotton core covered with polyester, these types of threads are suitable for using on the sewing machine. They are also available in large cones, which make them suitable for serger sewing.

Silk thread
Silk threads are ideal for sewing both silk and wool fabric, and for sewing by hand as they are soft and gentle to handle, and tend not to knot.

Machine embroidery floss
This is made from polyester or rayon, and has a high sheen that reflects the light. It is also available in cotton and even wool; these give a matte finish.

Metallic thread
This can be used for hand sewing and machining. If using a sewing machine, a special needle with a large eye is required to prevent the thread from breaking or shredding.

Wooly nylon
This is a soft, strong, thick thread that is used in the loopers of a serger. It is ideal for flatlocking and hemming as the loosely spun thread gives better coverage of the seam or edge. It is too thick to be used in serger needles.

Hand embroidery floss
These include twisted pearl cotton, loosely wound stranded threads that can be split and used as needed, soft embroidery floss, and tapestry yarns. These threads are too thick to go through machine needles, but they can be used in the loopers of sergers for decorative flatlocking and rolled hemming.

Bobbin fill
A fine thread, normally available in black or white and used in the bobbin of a sewing machine for machine embroidery, this thread reduces the bulk in an embroidered design. It can also be bought in pre-wound bobbins.

Basting thread
This soft cotton thread is weaker than general-purpose thread. It's therefore ideal for temporary hand sewing as it will break and not damage fabric when removed.

Topstitch thread
This is a stronger, thicker thread that gives a bolder finish. Use it for topstitching seams, hand sewing buttonholes, and for sewing on buttons. It should be used with a topstitch needle, as it has a larger eye to carry the thread, and with general-purpose thread wound onto the bobbin.

Choosing fabrics

A wide selection of fabrics in various textures and colors is available.

When selecting a fabric for your project, it's important to take the fabric's fiber content, texture (or "hand"), drape, color, and in some instances, the size of its print, or its horizontal stretch, into account. Once a piece of fabric is cut, it cannot be returned, and mistakes can be costly.

Commercial patterns contain valuable suggestions regarding which fabric types suit a garment's particular design. Check the back of the pattern envelope. You'll find a list of appropriate fabrics, their widths, and exactly how much fabric (what length) you will need to buy. Cotton and linen fabrics are available in standard widths of 36in (90cm) to 45in (120cm), and sometimes even 54in (130cm) and 60in (150cm). Woolens are most often woven on wider looms and normally measure about 60in (150cm) wide. Knit fabrics are usually available in widths from 56in (140cm) to 60in (150cm).

Don't trust your "eye" when selecting a fabric that must match the color of another garment. A shade of green, for example, can be difficult to visualize mentally. Green hues undergo subtle tonal changes depending upon whether they tend more toward the blue or the yellow in their composition. Bring the original garment with you to the fabric store, to be sure the colors are compatible.

Take time to decide on the perfect fabric for your needs. Lightweight corduroy, for example, is perfect for children's wear since it is very durable, and lightweight, silky knits will drape beautifully in the flowing lines of a dress.

Finally, when bringing your fabric home, and certainly when storing, roll the fabric instead of folding it. This will prevent creases that may be difficult to remove.

Attention to these details will ensure the success of your project, but coordinating a beautiful fabric in a color and texture that perfectly matches your garment's design will turn your project into a work of art.

Woven fabrics

Generally, medium-weight, woven fabrics are easy to handle and are the best choice for beginners. Stiff and bulky fabrics or those that are fine, with little body are more difficult to sew with.

COTTONS

These fabrics were traditionally made from 100% cotton but are often blended or even replaced with man-made fibers like polyester or rayon today.

Cotton A natural product of the cotton plant, cotton readily accepts colored dyes. Cotton has a tendency to shrink, so it's a good idea to preshrink before cutting out. Either pass over the fabric with a steam iron or launder beforehand. Cottons are usually cut on the grain for stability, but can be cut and sewn on the bias for ease of wear or design contrast.

Calico cotton A lightweight, plain-weave fabric, often with a printed pattern, this is appropriate for both casual clothing and children's wear since it launders well.

Chino A medium-weight, twill-weave cotton, with a slight sheen, most often dyed beige and often used for slacks. A heavier-weight chino, dyed in dark blue or black, is appropriate for work clothes.

Cotton batiste A fine, lightweight and sheer plain-weave cotton, this is ideal for children's wear, lingerie, handkerchiefs, and blouses. Cotton batiste is substantial enough to support hand or machine embroidery embellishments used in heirloom sewing techniques.

Cotton poplin's strength is derived from its tight weave.

Use weights instead of pins when cutting denim.

Consider the stripes and checks of gingham, and ensure these match at seams and openings.

Cotton broadcloth A medium weight fabric with a fine rib, available in pure cotton or a cotton-polyester blend. Broadcloth is commonly used for tailored blouses or shirts.

Cotton corduroy A cotton fabric, woven with a pile that is then cut to produce ribs. Available in different weights—lightweight, needle cord is excellent for children's clothing, tailored jackets and slacks; heavier, broad-wale corduroy is warm enough for outdoor sportswear. A variant, uncut corduroy, has a soft nap similar to velvet.

Cotton lawn Another lightweight, plain-weave cotton. Often quite sheer, this fabric is strong enough to hold pin tucks and smocking typical of children's wear. It's a good choice for summer blouses and dresses.

Cotton poplin A tightly woven cotton with a distinctive horizontal rib, this will withstand heavy wear and many launderings, and is appropriate for skirts, pants, and summer jackets.

Denim A heavyweight cotton usually dyed blue and constructed in a twill weave with white weft threads and blue warp threads. Suitable for work clothing, jeans, skirts, jackets, and children's clothes.

Gingham A medium-weight fabric available in pure cotton and also in cotton blends. The fabric's fibers are dyed beforehand and then woven to form checks or stripes.

Linen A crisp fabric, woven since ancient times from the natural fibers of the flax plant. The flax makes the fabric strong and absorbent, and also gives linen its high natural sheen. Like cotton, this natural fabric was traditionally used alone, but is now mixed with other fibers to alter its qualities. Spandex helps to reduce the wrinkling nature of linen. Silk and cotton may also be added.

Linen does wrinkle easily; however, this is considered part of its charm, and wrinkles are easily removed with a steam iron. The fabric accepts dyes very well and is available in a wide range of fashion colors. Natural-fiber or undyed linen is available in various weights and shades ranging from pale ivory to tan. "Pure white" linen is actually linen that has been heavily bleached. Because of its crispness, linen is ideal for tailored clothing, from lightweight blouses to heavyweight jackets.

Muslin An inexpensive, roughly woven cotton. The medium-weight variety is often used to construct "dummy" pants, or dress patterns, to check the fit before constructing the final garment in an expensive fabric. It is suitable for linings.

MICROFIBER FABRICS

These "miracle" microfiber fabrics are a modern invention. They are chemically produced filaments made of nylon and polyester. The microfibers that construct the final fabrics are exceedingly thin compared with conventional fabric threads, and therefore the weave is densely packed. The resulting fabrics share the texture and draping quality of natural fibers and are also lightweight, yet durable. Although the very fine fibers are ideal for emulating silk, they can be adapted for many uses.

Microfiber fabrics tend to be wind resistant as well as waterproof, so they are excellent for warm outdoor wear and impermeable rain gear. Microfibers are washable, but there is one note of caution: Because of their synthetic chemical composition, they tend to be heat sensitive, so care should be taken when pressing them or having them dry-cleaned.

Lightweight microfiber
Use this as an alternative to silk for lingerie and lightweight blouses.

Medium-weight microfiber
Use this for shirts and skirts where a soft draping quality is required, and for sports clothes (running and cycling).

Heavier microfiber
Choose this for jackets and weatherproof clothing.

SILK

A natural fiber, discovered 5,000 years ago by weavers in China who unwound the thin outer casings of silkworm larvae and used the thread to produce fabric of exceptional beauty and sheen. This can be emphasized with a satin weave cloth of 100% silk that is lovely to work with, but cheaper, synthetic fibers are often used to produce fabric of a similar appearance that does not handle as easily and can melt under the heat of the iron. Silk dyes well and is available in an array of vibrant colors, as well as muted tones. It is ideal for tailored blouses, bridal gowns, and other formal evening wear.

Crepe de Chine A lightweight, plain-weave silk with a matte texture and muted luster. Polyester imitations of this fabric are widely available. With a soft hand, it is ideal for lingerie, as well as for blouses and formal evening wear.

Microfiber drapes well, and does not cling or crease.

The color of dupion silk can vary depending on how light reflects on it, so cut all pieces in the same direction.

Dupion silk (also known as doupioni silk) A luxurious, heavyweight silk, made from weft threads spun from two cocoons, which produces irregular horizontal slubs. It is ideal for formal wear and bridal gowns.

Habotai silk (also called "China silk") A less expensive, lightweight, glossy silk variety. Habotai makes up the fine linings in coats and jackets, and can be printed with colorful patterns. It is a beautiful fabric for gorgeous, lightweight scarves.

Silk organza A sheer silk fabric, with highly twisted threads that make it very strong. Crisp, and with a sheen, it is used for bridal veils and gowns and other formal wear. Because of its fine weight, it is difficult to handle; one solution for achieving a perfect hemline is to roll and hand sew the hem. It is ideal as an underlining, as it is both thin and strong.

WOOL

A natural fiber processed from the fleece shorn from animals, mainly sheep. "Pure wool" is 100% wool; woolen blends, if so labeled, must contain at least 55% pure wool, which is then blended with other fibers, often silk. Woven wool textures tend to have bulk, enabling them to retain body heat. Conversely, wool also acts as insulation against heat and is a common fiber in clothing worn in desert areas. It is also naturally stain and wrinkle resistant. Wool fabrics vary enormously, depending on the breed from which the fibers come, whether they are used alone or mixed with other fibers, and how the fabric is constructed, making it possible to use woolen fabric for smart pants, coats, or chunky knitted sweaters.

Camel hair A fabric made of wool blended with natural hair fibers obtained from the camel's soft inner coat. Camel hair is a luxury fabric with a very soft hand that is ideal for overcoats. "Camel hair" often refers to the distinctive tan color of the natural hair.

Cashmere Another luxury fabric made from a blend of fine, undercoat hairs of the Kashmir goat. Soft and plush, cashmere is used for sweaters and other knitwear. Woven cashmere is ideal for overcoats and jackets.

Wool tartan A woolen, twill-weave fabric in multicolored plaid designs. Ancient Scottish clans designated particular tartan plaids within their own unique choice of colors. Wool tartan is ideal for forming and holding the pleated folds of kilts.

Not all wool plaids are "even plaids," with a symmetrical balance of colored threads. Colored-thread lines in other plaid designs may not be equally balanced, so it is important to take care when placing pattern pieces before you cut out sections of garments.

Worsted wool A more expensive woolen fabric, with a distinctive smooth surface. This fine wool responds well to steam pressing often required in couture tailoring techniques; it will also fall in softly draped lines.

Woven wool A plain weave, and a soft and warm fabric, woven wool is ideal for winter coats and jackets. Lightweight woolen blends are suitable for tailored suits and pants.

KNIT FABRICS

Knit fabrics are constructed with loops rather than warp and weft threads being woven together. The fibers used to make the threads/yarns for knit fabric may be natural wool, cotton, or synthetic, or various blends of these, allowing the creation of a multitude of knit fabrics.

Double knit A fabric in which the weave is the same on both sides. Available in cotton, cotton blends, wool, and other fibers, double-knit fabrics have moderate stretch. This should be taken into account when choosing a knit fabric for a garment. Medium-weight double knits are fine for pants and jackets; they will hold their shape but still have enough "give" for ease of movement. Lightweight double knits are good for dresses, since they will hold their shape and still drape well.

Interlock knit A fine, stable, single-knit fabric, normally manufactured in cotton or cotton-polyester blends. It is excellent for T-shirts, casual outerwear, and underwear.

Spandex A highly stretchable fiber, not used on its own, but blended with other knitted fibers to provide comfort and stretch. Formerly used only in lingerie and swimwear, spandex now finds its way into cotton and cotton-polyester blends for use in casual wear.

Sweatsuit fabric This heavyweight knit is warm and comfortable to wear, with a great deal of stretch, making it suitable for loose-fitting garments and sports clothing.

Tricot A delicate, warp-knit fabric, usually of nylon, with a crosswise stretch and no vertical stretch. Soft, smooth, and with good draping ability, it is excellent for lingerie.

Tartan yarns are dyed and then woven into the cloth in bands of color, creating plaids or checks.

Spandex is added to suiting fabrics to help garments retain their shape.

ANIMAL FABRICS

Either animal skin in origin or faux alternatives.

Faux fur Specially produced fabrics that imitate expensive animal fur. Because of the expertise in constructing these fabrics, many are difficult to distinguish from the "real thing," at least at first glance. Their value lies in that they offer a viable alternative to real fur. Constructing jackets and coats of faux fur requires special sewing techniques.

Faux suede A synthetic fabric, this is washable, durable, and ideal for jackets and tailored blazers. Since this fabric is an imitation of genuine leather suede, it will be necessary to use the same special sewing techniques required when handling genuine leather.

Leather Animal skins, or hides, that are suitable for clothing. Full-grain leather is now available in fashion colors. The availability of some skins may be restricted, however, because of animal-welfare laws. Leather requires special sewing techniques, and it may be necessary to purchase leather for a sewing project by the whole hide, rather than in specific yardage amounts.

SPECIAL FABRICS

Special-occasion wear makes use of the most luxurious and expensive fabrics. Fibers from all sources are constructed in a variety of ways to create special fabrics and garments.

Bouclé A wool or wool-blend fabric, and also a wool yarn, formed by a special process that makes loops. The woven bouclé wool surface has a nubby overall effect and is ideal for Chanel-type tailored jackets. Bouclé yarn is also suitable for knitted sweaters.

Chiffon An ultralight, sheer fabric, usually produced with silk threads. Reduced-cost versions are made from polyester. Chiffon has a fine draping quality and is greatly used in formal wear. This fabric can be difficult to handle. The usual voluminous hems found in evening dresses are best sewn by hand or with a serger.

Lace A fine, open cloth with a pattern, commonly used for evening and bridal wear, lingerie, and nightgowns, and as an edging for trimming garments. Lace is made with threads of silk, cotton, or synthetic fibers. Some laces are hand crocheted, and others are embroidered threads or cords on a net background.

Satin A fabric woven in silk, cotton, and synthetic fibers that has a shiny surface. Duchesse satin is a heavyweight, expensive variety and is used mostly for bridal dresses and formal evening wear.

Taffeta A plain-weave, silk fabric that is also produced in polyester and acetate. It is a crisp fabric, famous for the rustling sound it makes when worn in motion. Inexpensive versions are wonderful for children's "fancy dress" wear. It is usually dry-clean only.

Tulle A fine net, often of nylon, with a stiff feel. Tulle is most often used to make underskirts designed to support full-skirted bridal gowns or evening wear.

Velvet A tufted fabric, ideally woven in silk threads, but also manufactured from cotton, rayon, and synthetic fibers. The short thread loops are cut to form a dense pile, which lies in one direction. Rays of light cast on the slant of the pile are reflected from the fabric in varying shades of color, so care must be taken when cutting out pattern pieces. All of them have to be laid out in the same direction, so the garment will have a uniform color. Velvet also requires special pressing techniques.

INTERNAL FABRICS

Some specially created materials are designed for the internal construction of clothing and are not visible on the outside. These are essential in producing a perfect finish.

Interfacings fabrics Used to line and support the shape of garments. Haircloth interfacing is made from cotton blended with natural horse hair or synthetic fibers and is used mostly in professional tailoring techniques. Fusible interfacing, woven or bonded, and backed with a heat-fusing film, is available in various weights. Fusible fabrics are used to help shape and support garment details such as collars and necklines.

Stabilizers A wide variety of stabilizing materials is available. They are used to support fashion fabrics while those fabrics are being embellished. Choose a type to suit the project and fabric being used—tear-away, cut-away, and wash-away are all available in varying weights.

Leather is suitable for jackets, bags, belts, and upholstery.

Bouclé has an interesting surface texture.

All about commercial patterns

Commercial patterns were created to enable people to construct their own clothing at home. Produced in a range of sizes, they can be easily adapted to fit different figure shapes. With a vast range of designs available, from simple styles to fully tailored outfits, make your choice according to your level of sewing skills.

Why use a commercial pattern?

Commercial patterns provide an easy way to cut and make a garment that's just right for you.

Buying a store-bought pattern has many benefits. It contains information on everything you will need to know to construct your chosen design. The pattern will often include several different sizes, and you can combine elements from these to perfect your garment's fit. The outside of the envelope will provide you with a detailed guide about the fastenings and trimmings required, fabric suitability and how much to purchase, linings, and interfacings. Further details of construction can be found inside on the information sheet.

Commercial patterns

There are many popular names in the field of commercial patterns: Vogue, McCall's, Butterick, Simplicity, New Look, Burda, and Kwik Sew. The simplicity or complexity of available designs varies, ranging from a very simple dress for the beginner to a sophisticated couture design for the more experienced sewer.

The first patterns

The quality of commercial patterns has vastly improved since their introduction in the 1830s in England and France. Included in weekly or monthly magazines, the patterns were already cut out but had no printing on them and were made from poor-quality tissue paper. It wasn't until 1910 that detailed instruction sheets were included along with the pattern. There was little technical information provided to help cut and make the clothing—any information was printed in the magazine itself. The nineteenth-century home dressmaker needed a very high level of skills to interpret these early designs.

Selecting the correct size pattern

You may already have decided which pattern design you would like to make, but before you buy it, you will need to know which size to purchase. In order to do this, you will need to take some of your own basic measurements. Do not use your standard dress size (the one you use when you are shopping for clothes). Store dress sizes and commercial pattern sizes are different: a store size 10 may be a pattern size 12; however, most pattern companies do use the same body measurements (if you are a size 14 in Vogue, then you will be a 14 in McCall's). Pages 22–23 will explain how to measure yourself accurately. The main measurements to go by when buying a pattern are the bust and hip. Use the hip measurement when buying a skirt pattern and the bust for a top, a dress, or a garment that includes both measurements.

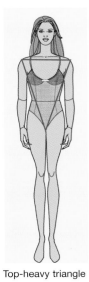

Top-heavy triangle

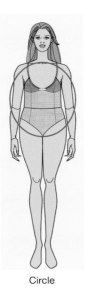

Circle

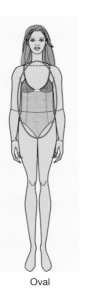

Oval

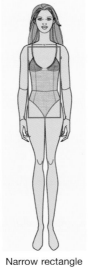

Narrow rectangle

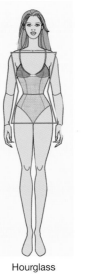

Hourglass

Bottom-heavy triangle

Body shape

An advantage of making your own clothes is that you can tailor them to your own body measurements; however, it's also important to select clothing styles that will work for you. When buying sewing patterns, think about your body shape and which clothing styles will complement it. Here, some general shapes are outlined which will help you to find the best look for your silhouette.

Top-heavy triangle

Choose smooth, clean lines above the waist to minimize the width across the shoulders and bust. Careful choice of collar and neckline, avoiding fussy details, is advisable. Plain fabrics or small prints and light textures are suitable.

Avoid cap sleeves, puff sleeves, and epaulettes. Keep sleeve designs simple. High-waist styles or those with a yoke should be avoided, as well as gathered waists and frills.

Circle (apple)

Choose tops, jackets, and dresses with pretty necklines that will draw the eye up and away from the waist. Scarves, jewelry, and shoes will also achieve this distraction. Choose tops and jackets in soft fabrics that layer over the waist.

Avoid tops and dresses that cling to the body. Do not draw attention to the waist with belts or styles that are obviously waist-focused. Keep clear of bright colors, especially in the middle of the body, and avoid cropped tops.

Oval

Choose styles that draw attention away from the center of the body and do not cut through the waist with a belt, band, or seam. Dresses or tunics are suitable, and skirts and pants worn with longer-length tops look good. Chunky necklaces and earrings draw attention away from the waist too.

Avoid figure-hugging T-shirts and styles that accentuate the waist, such as those with belts, and fitted or elasticized waistbands. Never tuck a shirt into a skirt or pants.

Tall, narrow rectangle, or column

Choose styles with detail at the bust and hip to create the illusion of shape. Choose fabrics with texture and pattern, such as chunky knitwear, fine wools, silks, and satins.

Avoid close-fitting pencil skirts, slim-shape straight pants, and figure-hugging T-shirts, which accentuate the long and narrow nature of this figure type.

Hourglass

Choose soft styles that drape over the body rather than tailored styles that may appear too large. Flowing fabrics in jersey knits or bias-cut styles will enhance an hourglass figure. Plain fabrics or fine patterns will be suitable.

Avoid crisp fabrics and boxy jackets, which are too angular for a curvy shape. Straight, shapeless dresses will do nothing for an hourglass shape. Large patterns, heavy textures, and checks add width to the body shape, so should be avoided.

Bottom-heavy triangle (pear)

Choose tops and jackets with details such as pockets, frills, and embroidery that will add interest and draw the eye up and away from the hip area. Careful attention to length is important, and horizontal lines should not cut across the hip, as this accentuates the problem.

Avoid halter neck and high-neck bodices, which emphasize narrow shoulders and a flat chest. Narrow, tapered-to-the-ankle pants and leggings are unflattering, especially when worn with baggy tops that make the silhouette appear larger and heavier.

How to measure accurately
The essential body landmarks.

When taking body measurements, it is extremely important to be accurate. A well-balanced, nicely-fitting garment could depend entirely on this. Keep your tape measure flat to the body and do not pull it tight or twist it. Try to keep all horizontal measurements level.

Tip
• Your working arm (depending on whether you are right or left handed) may have a greater circumference: up to an inch (2–3cm) more! If so, always use the larger measurement.

Photocopy this
Mark all your measurements down: remember to re-measure if your body changes shape over time.

MEASUREMENT CHART

Landmark	Standard Size US8/UK12	Personal Measurements
1 Bust	34¼in (87cm)	
2 Waist	26¾in (68cm)	
3 Hip	36¼in (92cm)	
4 CF neck to waist	12½in (32cm)	
5 CF shoulder to waist	13½in (34.5cm)	
6 Shoulder	3½in (9cm)	
7 Neck	14½in (37cm)	
8 C shoulder point to bust	9in (23cm)	
9 CB neck to waist	15¾in (40cm)	
10 CB shoulder to waist	16½in (42cm)	
11 Hip depth	8in (20.5cm)	
12 CF waist to floor	40½in (103cm)	
13 CF waist to knee	23in (58.5cm)	
14 Back	9¼in (23cm)	
15 CB waist to floor	41in (104cm)	
16 Upper arm	13½in (34cm)	
17 Arm length	22¼in (56.5cm)	

Getting started

Start by asking for help from a friend. It is virtually impossible to take accurate measurements by yourself. Use a dressmaker's measuring tape. Remove all of your outer clothing, but remain in your undergarments while measuring. Use the standard size US8/UK12 measurements (left) to compare with your own.

Use the diagrams provided opposite as a guide to where to take the measurements. These measurement points are called "body landmarks." Body landmarks can be indicated on your body by positioning sticky tape on your undergarments. Stand with your feet together while measuring.

Body landmarks

Body circumference:
- **1 Bust**—fullest part of the bust (keep level)
- **2 Waist**—1in. (2.5cm) above the navel
- **3 Hip**—fullest part of the body

Front bodice:
- **4 Center front (CF) neck**—length from front base of neck to waist
- **5 CF shoulder**—from base of neck at shoulder point to waist, over bust
- **6 Shoulder**—from base of neck to tip of shoulder

- **7 Neck**—around base of neck
- **8 Center shoulder to bust**—center of the shoulder to apex of the bust

Back bodice:
- **9 Center back (CB) neck**—neck to waist; find the large bone at the CB of your neck down to the CB waist
- **10 CB shoulder**—from base of neck at shoulder point to waist

Lower torso:
- **11 Hip depth**—from the CF waist point to the fullest part of the body
- **12 CF waist to floor**—from the CF waist to floor

- **13 CF waist to knee**—CF waist to center of knee
- **14 Back**—lower torso (bust line to waist)
- **15 CB waist to floor**—CB at waist to floor

Arm:
- **16 Upper arm**—circumference of your upper arm
- **17 Arm length**—shoulder to wrist measured with arm slightly bent

When measuring
Get the help of a friend when taking your body measurements. It's not possible to be accurate if you're bending down and twisting to maneuver the tape measure.

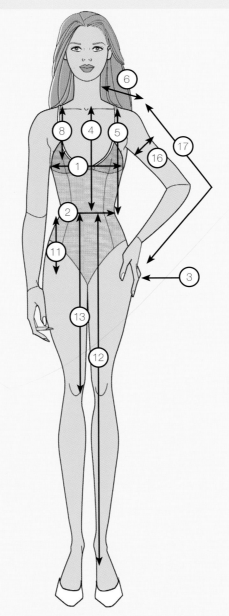

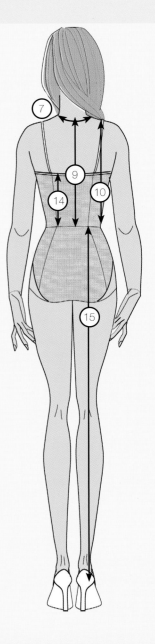

Children

Follow the same method of measuring accurately for a child as for an adult. Have the child remove any outer clothing. Again, remember you are measuring the body, not the clothes.

Tie a piece of elastic or cord around the waist. Have the child bend sideways—the elastic will settle at the waist.

Children's clothing is quicker and easier to construct than adults', mainly because the designs are often simpler to allow for unrestricted movement and growth, and to help younger children dress themselves. The patterns are generally flat in construction, not needing any dart shaping until the child reaches puberty (about 10 for girls and 12 for boys), when the bust or chest, waist, and hips become more defined.

Children's "body landmarks" and where they are found

Below are the "body landmarks," where you should take measurements on the child's body. The chest, waist, and hip measurements are the most important. Measurements marked with a * are needed to purchase a pattern.

- **1** *Breast or chest
- **2** *Waist
- **3** *Hips
- **4** *Center back (neck to waist)
- **5** *Height
- **6** Shoulder
- **7** Crotch depth
- **8** Inside leg
- **9** Outside leg
- **10** CB (waist to floor)
- **11** CB (waist to knee)
- **12** Arm length

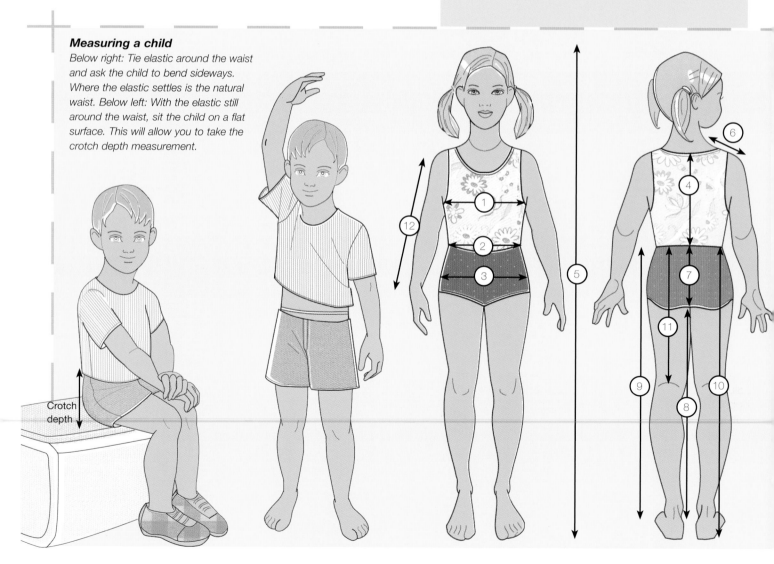

Measuring a child

Below right: Tie elastic around the waist and ask the child to bend sideways. Where the elastic settles is the natural waist. Below left: With the elastic still around the waist, sit the child on a flat surface. This will allow you to take the crotch depth measurement.

Crotch depth

What size pattern should you purchase?

Children's sizing is classified into the stages of a child's growth. The first "children's" size is from two years, when a child is standing and no longer wearing a diaper. This sizing category lasts up to age six. "Boys' and girls'" sizing starts from age seven, when their growth remains virtually the same up to age 10 years. It is important to remember that these size classifications are only a general guide, since all children grow at different rates.

Children's size charts

Children's pattern measurements

Size	X-Small	Small		Medium		Large
	2	3	4	5	6	6X
Breast or chest	21in (53cm)	22in (56cm)	23in (58cm)	24in (61cm)	25in (64cm)	25½in (65cm)
Waist	20in (51cm)	20½in (52cm)	21in (53cm)	21½in (55cm)	22in (56cm)	22½in (57cm)
Hip	–	-	24in (61cm)	25in (64cm)	26in (66cm)	26½in (67cm)
Back waist length	8½in (22cm)	9in (23cm)	9½in (24cm)	10in (25.5cm)	10½in (27cm)	10¾in (27.5cm)
Approximate height	35in (89cm)	38in (97cm)	41in (104cm)	44in (112cm)	47in (119cm)	48in (122cm)

Girls' and boys' pattern measurements

Size	Small	Medium		Large		X-Large
	7	8	10	12	14	16
Breast or chest	26in (66cm)	27in (69cm)	28½in (73cm)	30in (76cm)	32in (81cm)	34in (86.5cm)
Waist	23in (58cm)	23½in (60cm)	24½in (62cm)	25½in (65cm)	26½in (67cm)	27½in (68.5cm)
Hip	27in (69cm)	28in (71cm)	30in (76cm)	32in (81cm)	34in (87cm)	36in (91.5cm)
Back waist length	11½in (29.5cm)	12in (31cm)	12¾in (32.5cm)	13½in (34.5cm)	14½in (36cm)	15in (38cm)
Approximate height	50in (127cm)	52in (132cm)	56in (142cm)	58½in (149cm)	61in (155cm)	61½in (156cm)

Measurement chart

In the sizing table, right, the measurements marked with a * are needed to purchase a pattern. Measurements 6 to 12 indicate the alterations required to achieve a personal fit. Children grow very fast, so it is important to measure them frequently. They may grow in height and keep the same circumference or the other way around. As a general rule, when choosing a pattern, if a child is between sizes it is advisable to choose the larger size and alter it to fit.

Because children's sizes are classified differently than adult sizes, you'll first need to measure your child and fill in the column on the right. Then, using a pattern appropriate to your child's age, fill out the pattern measurements in the left-hand column and compare the two.

Photocopy this
MEASUREMENT CHART

Landmark	Standard Size	Personal Measurement
1 * Breast or chest		
2 * Waist		
3 * Hips		
4 * Center back (neck to waist)		
5 * Height		
6 Shoulder		
7 Crotch depth		
8 Inside leg		
9 Outside leg		
10 CB (waist to floor)		
11 CB (waist to knee)		
12 Arm length		

Buying a commercial pattern

Once you have measured yourself accurately, you can start shopping for your pattern.

Many department stores and chain stores have a notions department. Here you will find large catalogs produced by the different pattern companies. Some catalogs are published seasonally or twice yearly. The prices of patterns can vary from one company to another, ranging from $3.40 to $30.00.

Pattern catalogs

Pattern catalogs are divided into sections, with tabs to help you locate a pattern easily. Take some time to look through these tabs because the categories will guide you through women's patterns, figure types, designer labels, men's patterns, and children's patterns. The catalogs usually indicate the skill level needed for a specific pattern. Some pattern companies include costumes, accessories, home furnishings, and patterns for special occasions such as christenings and weddings.

Purchasing a pattern online

Technology has provided new ways to purchase paper patterns. There are many online pattern companies and sewing stores to choose from. They range from companies selling patterns to be delivered by mail to those where you can download and print the pattern immediately. Many companies have chat rooms where home sewers can exchange sewing experience with each other, along with photos of completed projects. You can also join clubs and receive regular updates on special offers. Some costume museums and designer labels have patterns to download, often for free!

Download pros and cons

There are advantages and disadvantages to downloading patterns. The most obvious advantage is that you receive your pattern right away. However, the big disadvantage is that unless you have a very large printer or access to one, you must painstakingly glue your pattern together—and the more complicated designs take a lot of time and patience.

Printing and assembling your downloaded pattern

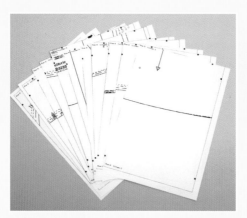

1 The downloaded pattern prints on your normal home printer on 8½ x 11in (21.5 x 28cm) sheets with a heavy black border. On each sheet are column and row numbers along with small black boxes to help when matching up the sheets.

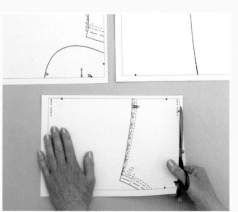

2 First, organize and divide the sheets of paper by rows, numbers, or letters and cut off the margins on the top and left sides.

3 Now you are ready to glue the sheets together side-by-side to form rows. It is important to pay special attention to matching the black boxes. Be as accurate as possible.

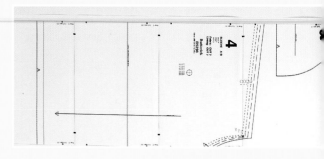

Tab categories

- Evening and bridal
- Dresses
- Very easy Vogue dresses
- Designer sportswear
- Sportswear
- Very easy sportswear
- Jackets and coats
- Tops and blouses
- Skirts and pants
- Vintage Vogue
- Today's fit
- The Vogue woman
- Maternity
- Kids
- Men
- Fashion accessories
- Vogue doll collection
- Crafts and home decorating

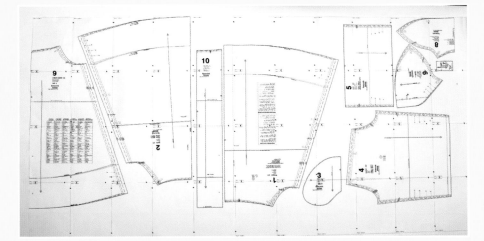

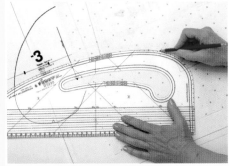

5 Once the pattern is complete, it is a good idea to trace it onto pattern tracing paper. This will make the pattern easier to pin to your fabric because pattern tracing paper is made for that purpose.

4 Once all the rows are finished, paste them together lengthwise. The pattern is now complete.

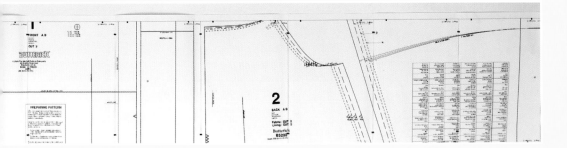

Understanding your pattern

Following the detailed instructions outside and inside the pattern envelope takes the guesswork out of making your garment.

When you look at your pattern for the first time, take some time to look over the information on the back and on the pattern information sheet inside.

The back of the envelope

Commercial pattern envelopes hold a variety of information:

• Silhouette key, indicating the body type the pattern is recommended for.

• A short description of the designs included.

• Suggested fabrics and notions for use with each garment. The pattern may also suggest that the design is unsuitable for certain fabrics. For jersey fabrics you will find a stretch guide on how much elasticity is recommended for the design.

• Detailed diagrams of the garments showing both front and back views.

• A guide to the amount of fabric you will need to purchase for your chosen garment. The diagram to the right shows where to look for information on how much fabric, lining, and interfacing to purchase in the correct fabric width.

• A guide to the specific details of each garment.

Silhouette key —

Description —

Suggested fabrics and notions —

Front and back views of the garments —

Guide to the quantity of fabric required —

Garment details —

The pattern envelope

The back of the envelope carries a lot of essential information, including how to calculate the amount of fabric you will need.

Understanding the information on the pattern pieces

All commercial patterns have essential information printed on the pattern pieces. It is important to transfer this information from the paper pattern onto the fabric. There are many different ways to do this, and methods vary for different fabric types (see pages 34–41).

Printed on each pattern piece, you will find a style number, a name that identifies the pattern piece, and the number of pieces to cut along with information indicating which kind of fabric to cut the pattern out of, i.e., fabric, lining, or interfacing.

The triangle shapes are called "notches." These are symbols for matching seams. Notches can also mark the front and back of the pattern and indicate where a zipper will finish.

This picture shows a back notch. The small circles indicate a "matching point" that will correspond to an adjoining pattern (in this case to the bodice armhole).

The picture shows a front notch.

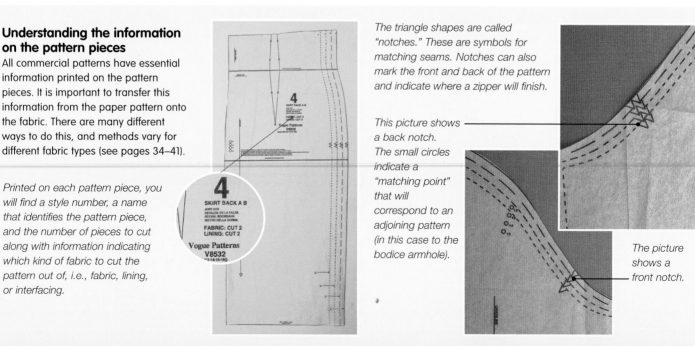

The information sheet

This sheet provides detailed instructions on which pattern pieces are needed to make your chosen style and supplies information on body measurements, cutting instructions, and seam allowances. It also gives specific pattern layouts for different widths of fabric. The information is often pictorial, making it very easy to follow.

Line drawings show the styles.

Body measurements (see page 24).

Fabric cutting layout plans for style and fabric width.

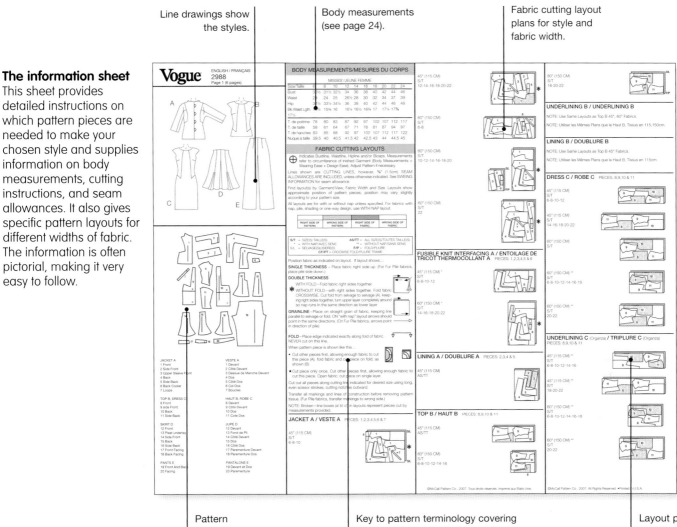

Pattern pieces are identified.

Key to pattern terminology covering grain, cutting on fold, right and wrong side of fabric (see pages 34–41).

Layout plans for interfacings and linings.

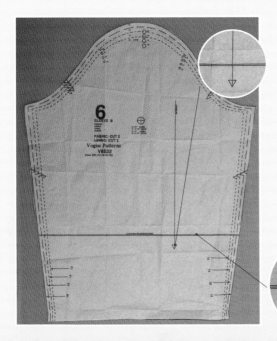

This symbol indicates the grain line. The arrow at one end points in the direction of the pile when using fabric with a nap, the smooth or right side running in the direction of the arrow.

This double line indicates where a pattern can be shortened and lengthened. Remember that you may need to purchase more fabric if you lengthen a pattern.

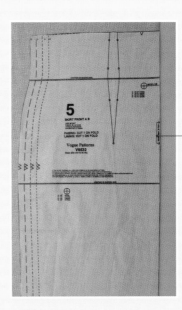

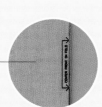

This symbol indicates the pattern pieces that need to be placed on the fabric's fold.

Preparing a commercial pattern

The following pages explain how to prepare your commercial pattern for use.

When preparing a commercial sewing pattern for use, there are three crucial factors that you should know about: "ease allowance"—vital for the body to move within the garment; "fit"—whether the garment is tight or loose; and "style"—the design of the garment itself. These three elements must be considered when you are altering an existing pattern to fit your own size accurately.

You should have purchased the pattern size closest to your body measurements. Use your hip measurement for a skirt, and your bust measurement for a top or a dress. If the size chart on the back of the pattern corresponds to your own body measurements, this makes things a little easier. If, however, your measurements are different from the size chart, you are advised to pick a larger size (it's easier to make a pattern smaller than it is to make it larger). This means you may need to make some alterations to your pattern in order to create the fit you want.

If you do need to make alterations to your pattern, you will need to use your body measurements and measure the pattern pieces and compare the two. You will find that the measurements on the pattern pieces are more generous than those shown on the pattern sizing. This extra allowance is called ease (see opposite), and it is already included in the pattern.

Cutting the pattern pieces out

Before you can measure your pattern pieces, you need to identify them and cut them apart. When you first take your pattern out of the envelope, start by looking for all the pattern pieces with the letter that corresponds to your chosen garment. There are often several styles in one envelope, which can be confusing, so locate your pieces and check them against the list on the instruction sheet to make sure you have them all.

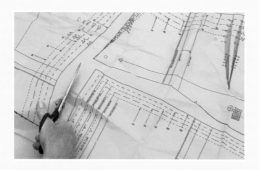

1 Once you have identified the relevant pattern pieces for your garment, cut them apart from the others.

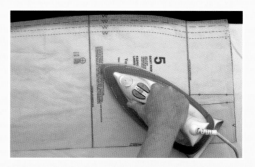

2 Before you accurately cut out the pattern pieces, first press all the creases and folds out of the paper with a warm, dry iron.

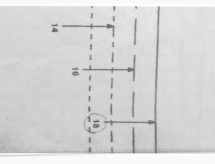

3 Many patterns have several sizes marked on each pattern piece, so you will need to look for your size. The sizes are marked by different patterns of dot–and–dash lines. It helps to highlight the correct size at this point, making identification clearer.

4 Only after you have checked that you have the right size and line, should you cut out the pattern. When cutting out your pattern, it is important to cut outside the line and to be as accurate as possible.

What is ease and why do we need it?

There are two different types of ease, "wearing ease" and "design ease." Wearing ease in a garment is essential for movement. If the pattern didn't include wearing ease, you would not be able to sit, walk, or move when wearing it because the pattern would fit your body measurements exactly. On page 32 is a design ease allowance chart. The ease measurements listed are the amounts that have been added to a pattern to achieve a certain fit, i.e., close-fitting, loose-fitting, and so on.

Wearing ease chart

The ease allowances in the chart below are a minimum ease measurement in a woven fabric (fabric without stretch). They have already been added to the pattern—so don't be seduced by your body measurements and reduce your pattern size!

Refer to your personal measurement chart (on page 22). You will need to add ease to your body measurements in order for them to correspond with those on the pattern. In the chart below you can record your measurements plus ease.

Photocopy this

WEARING EASE CHART

Landmark		Ease to add	Total measurement and ease
1	Bust	$2^{7}/_{8}$ in (7.3cm)	
2	Waist	$^{3}/_{4}$ in (2cm)	
3	Hip	$^{3}/_{4}$ in (2cm)	
4	Crotch Depth	$^{1}/_{2}$ in (1.3cm)	
5	Crotch Length	$1^{1}/_{2}$ in (3.8cm)	
6	Wrist	$^{2}/_{3}$–1in (1.5–2.5cm)	

Garment style

Consider the design style itself when checking the measurements and "fit" of your garment. The garment may contain styles that don't correspond to the points from which the body measurements have been taken. For example, with a dropped shoulder, the pattern shoulder measurement will be very long. This is because the armhole seam has been dropped and the shoulder extended to achieve this style. For a large or cutaway neckline, the shoulder measurement will be short. This is because the neckline does not start at the base of the neck. So, be aware that some of your measurements may differ from those on the pattern and take this into account. Another relevant example is a dropped or low waist line on pants or skirt (sometimes called hipster). Don't compare this measurement with your natural waist measurement, because the garment is not worn on the waist.

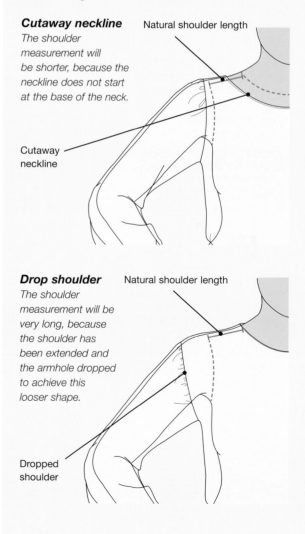

Cutaway neckline
The shoulder measurement will be shorter, because the neckline does not start at the base of the neck.

Natural shoulder length

Cutaway neckline

Drop shoulder
The shoulder measurement will be very long, because the shoulder has been extended and the armhole dropped to achieve this looser shape.

Natural shoulder length

Dropped shoulder

Design ease

Design ease is the amount of fullness added to a garment in addition to wearing ease that gives the garment the look that the designer is aiming for. The chart on the right explains the general silhouette classifications that pattern companies use to help clarify how a garment will fit the body. The first column describes the fit and the next three specify the amount of ease that has been added to the pattern to achieve that fit, according to the particular garment type. It's important never to borrow fullness from the design ease in order to accommodate wearing ease because you'll lose the intended shape of the garment.

Ease allowances (not applicable for garments designed for stretchable knit fabrics)

Silhouette	Bust area		
	Dresses, tops, shirts, vests, blouses	Jackets	Coats
		Lined/unlined	
Close fitting	0–2⅞in (0–7.3cm)	Not applicable	Not applicable
Fitted	3–4in (7.5–10cm)	3¾–4¼in (9.5–10.7cm)	5¼–6¾in (13.3–17cm)
Semi fitted	4⅛–5in (10.4–12.5cm)	4⅜–5¾in (11.1–14.5cm)	6⅞–8in (17.4–20.5cm)
Loose fitting	5⅛–8in (13–20.5cm)	5⅞–10in (14.8–25.5cm)	8⅛–12in (20.7–30.5cm)
Very loose fitting	Over 8in (over 20.5cm)	Over 10in (25.5cm)	Over 12in (30.5cm)

Your measurements + wearing ease + design ease = silhouette

Silhouette classifications

You can sometimes find these silhouette classifications in pattern catalogs to help you to understand the garment silhouette.

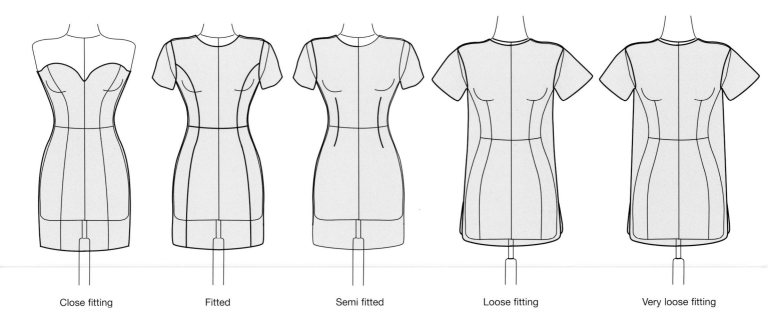

Close fitting   Fitted   Semi fitted   Loose fitting   Very loose fitting

Measuring the pattern

Measuring the pattern accurately enables you to check the fit of your garment. General pattern points to check for fit are as follows:

Bust + ease
Waist + ease
Hips + ease
Shoulder
Shoulder neck point to bust point (apex)
CB length
CF length
Side seams
Sleeve length

Compare the pattern measurements to your measurements and add ease where necessary. (See chart on page 22). Remember that when you measure the front and back waist, hips, and bust on a pattern you must double the measurement, because you have measured only half of the pattern.

How to check a skirt waist for fit

Before starting to measure your pattern, the seam allowance must be marked out with a seam guide or ruler. In this example, the pattern includes a seam allowance of ⅝in (1.5cm).

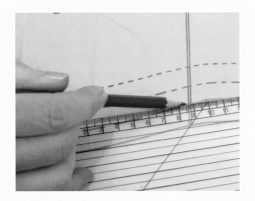

1 Measure inward around your pattern from the line indicating your chosen size and mark this with a pencil.

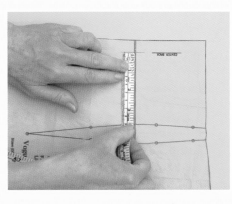

2 Once the seam allowance has been marked out, measure the waist, excluding the seam allowance and the dart. Start from the CB (or CF) up to the side of the dart.

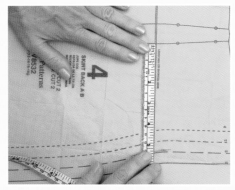

3 Now continue from the other side of the dart to the side seam stitching line. Double the measurement to obtain the total width of the back. Do the same for the front.

A quicker method

Fold out the dart and measure from CB waist to the side seam stitching line all in one movement.

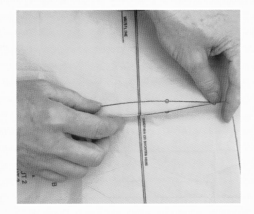

1 Start by folding out the dart.

2 Pin the dart closed and measure straight across from the CB to the side seam allowance.

Preparing your fabric

Be aware of your fabric's structure before you cut out your garment.

You will need to consider your fabric carefully before you start to cut out your garment. Information inside the commercial pattern will give pointers regarding layouts for different widths of fabric, whether to cut in single or double layers, and on matching patterns when using a non-standard fabric such as a plaid, print, or stripe. Unless you are using a pattern designed specifically for the bias, where instructions will be supplied, understanding the correct grain, if a fabric has skewed, and finding the right and wrong sides of the fabric are the first steps toward laying out your pattern pieces and cutting them out.

Fabric grain

Woven fabrics are made up of lengthwise warp yarns and crosswise weft yarns. The selvages are the finished edges of the fabric where the weft yarns double back on themselves during the weaving process. In garment construction, the "straight grain" is the most commonly used grain, which runs parallel to the selvages and when laying out the pattern pieces, up and down the garment. This is because the lengthwise warp grain is stronger, with less stretch. The crosswise weft, woven from weaker or "filler" yarns, usually has some give in it. You can use a fabric's grain to your advantage. For example, if you wanted to create more volume, you could consider changing the grain so that the warp runs crosswise instead of lengthwise. The true bias is at a 45-degree angle to the straight grain.

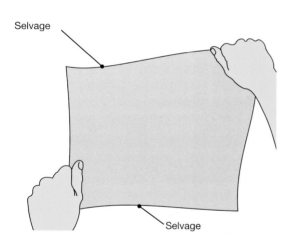

Selvage

Selvage

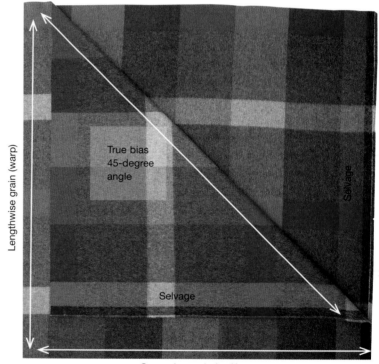

Lengthwise grain (warp)

True bias 45-degree angle

Selvage

Selvage

Crosswise grain (weft)

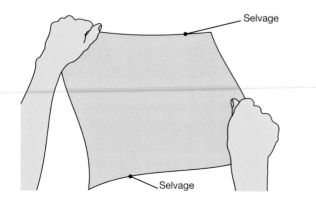

Selvage

Selvage

Selvage

Using the bias

If you wanted to achieve a very soft draped look to a garment, you would use the bias grain. Caution should be used when using the bias, since in this direction the fabric becomes stretchy and tricky to sew. Its hanging weight pulls the fabric down, making it longer and narrower than the original cut proportion. The iconic dresses of the 1930s used bias grain to achieve the streamlined silhouette that clung to the natural contours of the body.

Making the fabric end straight

Straightening the ends of your fabric will help to line up the grain correctly.

Most pattern layouts are cut with the fabric folded in half in the same direction as the straight grain. However, before you pin your paper pattern pieces onto the fabric, it is important to check that the grain is straight.

There are two methods that can be used to do this, but they work only on woven cloth. Pulling a thread is by far the gentlest method. If the fabric has a smooth surface, you can see the pulled thread. If the fabric is loosely woven, when a thread is pulled and removed, a gap is created indicating a straight edge. The tearing method may create distortion and stretch to the edge of the fabric, so always start with the gentler method and proceed to other methods if that does not work. If at any time the fabric starts to snag, run, or damage the warp threads—stop. It's a good idea to test your fabric first for suitability.

Pulling a thread

1 It may be necessary to make a small snip in the selvage to get hold of a thread.

2 Try to isolate a single weft thread—then pull it: This creates a puckered line across the width.

3 Continue to pull the thread all the way along, from selvage to selvage. If it is difficult to see the pulled thread, you may have to repeat this.

4 For a straight edge, cut parallel to the line that has been created.

Tearing the fabric

1 First snip through the selvage—this makes tearing easier.

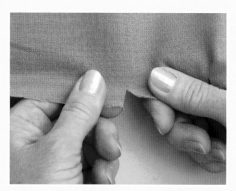

2 Start tearing. If there is any resistance, it is best to stop. Some fabrics, although woven, are not suitable, because of the weave or the finish on the fabric's surface. You cannot tear jerseys or knits.

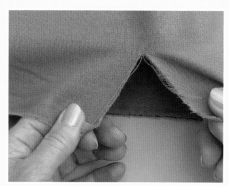

3 Continue tearing. Once you have a straight end, press your fabric with a warm iron.

Skewed fabric

By straightening the ends of your fabric, you will see if it has skewed. Skewing is when the warp and weft are not at true right angles to each other. Sometimes fabrics can become skewed or pulled off grain during the finishing process. Skewing often happens when the fabric is rolled onto a bolt using uneven tension.

Fixing a skewed woven fabric

1 Sometimes a skewed fabric can be fixed if its grain isn't too "off." First, straighten your fabric ends (see page 35). Next, folding the fabric in half lengthwise, align the ends and selvages. Test your fabric with a moderately hot steam iron to ensure that it does not stain or scorch and then try to press "the skew" away. You may need to machine- or hand-baste the edges to keep the fabric in place while doing this. Avoid pressing the folded edge flat, since this may be difficult to remove later.

2 Alternatively, you could try folding the fabric in half, matching selvages and aligning the ends as before. Baste if necessary at the ends and selvages to keep it steady. Next, dampen the fabric, place it between damp sheets, and leave it to dry naturally. Do not hang the fabric while it is drying—it is important that it remains flat and supported to avoid stretching.

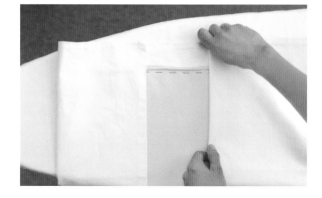

Skewed jersey and tubular knit fabrics

Knits or jerseys are constructed differently from woven fabrics. They are made up of rows of interlocking loops and often have no selvages. If a knit fabric has skewed, it must be treated differently from a woven fabric.

How to straighten a flat knit

First, fold your fabric in half, lining up the lengthwise edge; be aware of the knit stitches and try to keep them parallel. Once this is achieved, pin or baste the fabric in position and gently steam. Be careful not to steam the fold or pins into the fabric, since this could leave a permanent mark.

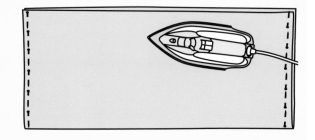

How to straighten a tubular knit

Follow the same method as for a flat knit, but cut one side following a knit grain line. This will release one side so you can realign and straighten the fabric.

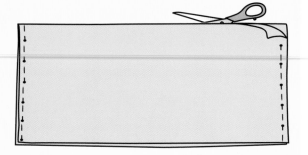

Stripes

You can create interesting effects using striped and printed fabrics. When using a striped fabric, or a fabric with a prominent lengthwise weave or relief, the visual effect can be quite dramatic. Consider the effect that will be created when adjoining seams meet on your garment.

Using striped fabric

When using a striped fabric—before you lay out your pattern pieces—it's important that you consider the way the grain (and therefore the stripes) will run on the finished garment. Crosswise, lengthwise, or on the bias? This decision will affect the way the pattern works when the fabric meets at the seams. This also applies to check fabrics.

Striped fabric layout
For this pattern, the stripes will need to be matched vertically from the bodice to the skirt. A stripe should be central at the CF or either side of the CF, depending on the design.

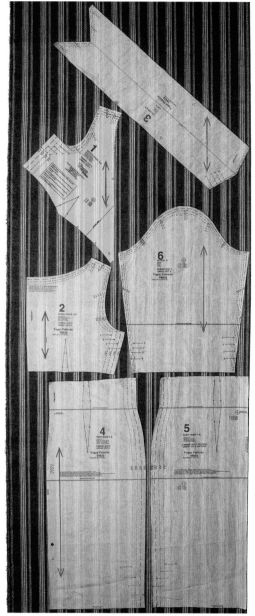

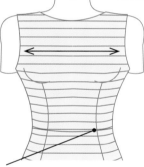

When using striped fabric with the grain (and therefore the stripes) running lengthwise, you need to consider how the stripes will meet at a dart.

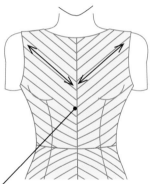

When diagonal stripes (bias grain) meet at a seam, they will form chevrons down the seam. You will have to plan this carefully when laying out the pattern pieces.

When crosswise stripes meet at a seam, they will change angle slightly as they pass around the body, according to the shaping of the garment.

Identifying the correct side

There is no rule that you have to use the right side of a fabric. You may prefer the wrong side but, remember that the right side often has a finish to help resist soiling. Once you've identified the correct (right) side of your fabric, a small chalk mark in the seam allowance is a useful reminder. If the correct side is not obvious, here are some clues to help you choose:

- The selvage is a good place to start— smoothness indicates the right side, rough the wrong.

- The way the fabric is folded when it's purchased. Cottons and linens are folded with the right side out; woolens with the wrong side out.
- If fabric is purchased on a roll, the right side is inside.
- Sometimes the fabric finish is a good indicator: shiny or dull, smooth or rough.
- Prints are often easier to identify, because they are usually sharper on the right side.
- Plaids can be brighter on the right side, or the line can be more defined.

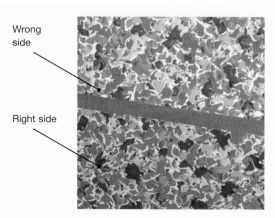
Wrong side

Right side

The right side of a print is often darker.

Directional prints

If you're using a printed fabric, it's important that you know how to recognize one-way or two-way prints and how to use them. It is very important to consider your print before laying out your pattern pieces. Notice if there is a distinctive top and bottom to the design.

Directional print layout ▶

This is a two-way floral print, with no defined top or bottom. If the print is very pronounced, matching the side seams is a good idea. Make sure you match the stitch line, not the pattern edge. Note how the thin, see-through paper of a commercial pattern makes matching the design much easier.

◀ One-way print

This paisley fabric has a very clear top and bottom to the design and must be treated as a one-way print, whichever direction you decide to use. When laying your pattern pieces out, you will have to place the top of all the pattern pieces facing the same way.

◀ Two-way print

In this print, the flower design has been placed going both up and down the fabric. You are not restricted and can use either end for the top of your garment. You will still need to assess if matching the print is necessary.

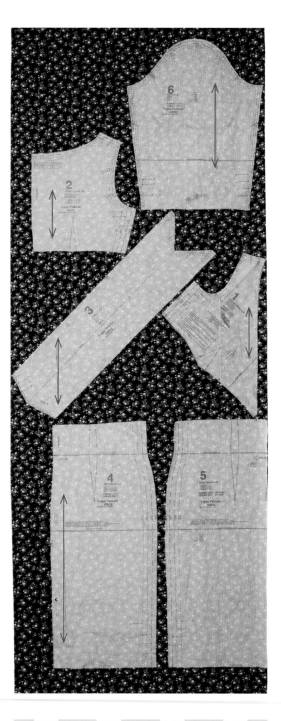

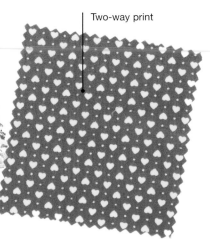

Two-way print

One-way print

Tip

• When cutting fabric, use a large, flat surface at a convenient height. Cut with long-bladed scissors or use a rotary cutter with a self-healing cutting mat beneath it.

Napped, or pile, fabrics

A napped or pile fabric has a raised fuzzy texture with a definite direction to its surface; it is sometimes called a "one-way fabric." Examples of this are corduroy, velvet, velveteen, suede cloth, and fake fur. When you run your hand along in one direction the fabric is smooth and shiny, and in the other it is rough and dull.

When pattern pieces are laid on a one-way fabric, it is again important that they lie in the same direction. You can clearly see the effect of a one-way fabric when it has been cut incorrectly.

Pile fabric layout ▶

This is an example of a one-way layout, appropriate for napped and pile fabrics and one-way prints. All the tops of the pattern pieces are facing toward the top end of the fabric, and because you cannot turn the pattern pieces around to make them fit more economically, you may need to buy more fabric.

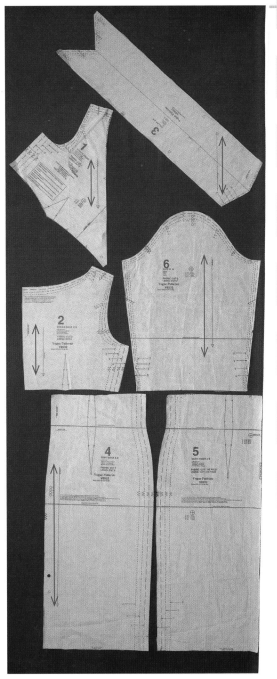

Fabric preparation tips

- Check the fabric for flaws before cutting out any garment or project. You may be able to work around small problems but it's best to inspect the fabric before you make your purchase.
- Preshrink the fabric by washing it in the way the garment will eventually be laundered, if appropriate, or by steaming it with an iron—by hovering lightly over the surface of the fabric.
- Prewash fabrics and lace or ribbon embellishments before starting construction to ensure that the colors do not bleed when washed as a completed garment.

| Suede

Test napped fabric for shading

When the nap is running upward, the color will be richer; when running downward, the fabric feels smooth but the color will be less vibrant. This velvet clearly shows the difference.

Using a plaid fabric

The range of plaid fabrics is vast. Apart from the difference in the scale of the squares themselves, you will find that certain designs are more even, whereas others have a more irregular arrangement of squares and bars.

An even plaid will be easier to use because it is symmetrical. If you spread your folded fabric out on a table, turn down one corner, and the squares match, then the plaid is even.

An uneven plaid will take more planning when aligning the pattern pieces on the fabric and will require extra material for a layout similar to one-way fabrics.

Cutting plaid

When cutting a plaid, as with stripes, you must consider how the plaid will match when the seams meet. You may want the plaid to meet in horizontal stripes or perhaps to chevron for a dramatic effect. Think about where you want the bars to be placed on the body. The image to the right is an example of a central arrangement. The same stripe or bar runs through the CF and CB, matching at the shoulder seam. The stripe on the sleeve head will match the stripe on the bodice armhole front and back. It is always safer to cut plaids in a single layer, rather than with the fabric folded, so that you can see both sides to measure and match the plaid exactly.

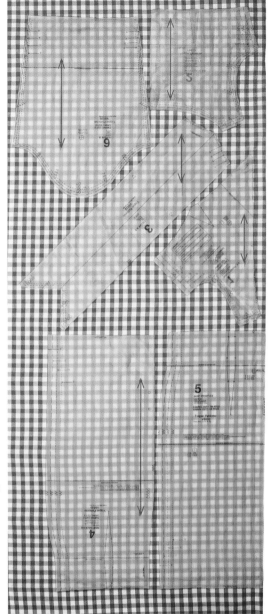

Even plaid

An even plaid makes laying out pattern pieces easy. You still have to consider matching horizontal and vertical lines, but pattern pieces can be turned to minimize fabric wastage. Although these pieces are facing in opposite directions, key points, such as hip lines, still match up.

Uneven plaid

When using an uneven plaid, matching the strong horizontal and vertical lines needs more careful consideration. Here, a stripe in the design has been used to align the hip line.

Tartan

Using bias and silk fabrics

Extra care and patience is required when cutting a garment on the bias. Bias-cut designs are deceiving, often looking simple, with few seams. Silks or silky fabrics are favored for their expensive look and the natural drape that they provide—but they are often fine and slippery, and require a very light touch and minimal handling in both the cutting out and sewing.

Only use a commercial pattern designed specifically for the bias, because extra width has been provided for in the pattern to allow for the weight and stretch of the bias fabric. The amount of width needed will vary from one silk to another. If your garment is too tight, it will pucker and twist.

When cutting silk on the bias, treat it as a one-way layout (see page 38). This will minimize the danger of cutting different grains, which will react in different ways to cause twisting or puckering and also to protect against shading (when opposing grains make a fabric appear a different color).

For the best results, do not fold the fabric; cut out in a single thickness, and place a layer of pattern tracing paper under the silk. The silk will cling to the paper, helping to keep it stable while it is cut out with a pair of sharp shears. Serrated scissors can also be helpful for cutting out silk.

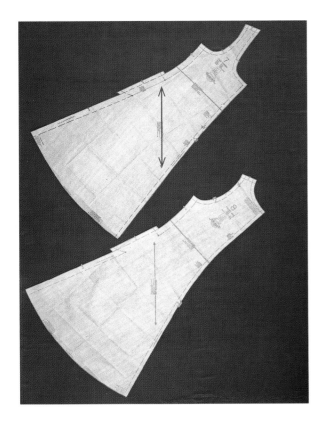

◄ *Bias dress pattern layout on silk*

This dress has both CF and CB seams. The commercial pattern supplies only two half-garment patterns, so another pattern layout will be required with the pieces placed as opposites. Keep the tops of the pattern pieces pointing in the same direction, because the silk can behave differently if the grain direction changes.

Maintaining proportions when working with bias fabrics

To counteract the narrowing qualities of fabric used on the bias, you must add 1in (2.5cm) to the existing seam allowances at the side seams. This extra width helps to counteract the effect of the hanging weight, pulling the fabric down and making it longer and narrower.

Before sewing the pattern pieces together, cut the garment out and pin it onto a dress form, and then leave it to hang overnight or longer. In this time, the weight of the fabric will draw the dress downward, making it narrower. If you temporarily hand baste the side seams onto the dress form, this will keep the slippery fabric in place until it can be stitched on the machine.

Leave the garment to hang on the dress form again, before leveling out the hem and stitching.

Pinning, marking, and cutting out

It is important that you have a large clear surface on which to prepare your pattern.

You need to maintain complete accuracy when placing your pattern pieces before pinning them onto your fabric. Any discrepancies to the grain or movement that adds or removes fabric could ruin the fit of your garment and, at this stage, be difficult to detect and alter. Marking the pattern information such as notches, darts, and pockets onto the fabric accurately is vital, and you must consider the best tools for the job. This will be entirely determined by the fabric you have chosen. Simple sizing alterations suitable for commercial patterns, such as lengthening and shortening the bodice, sleeve, skirt, dress, and pants, will help provide your pattern with a more accurate fit, providing the professional finish that you desire.

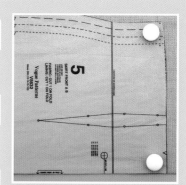

Tip
• Placing weights on pattern pieces before pinning or drawing around them is a useful tip. Weights can be purchased from sewing stores, or simply use any small, reasonably heavy item close at hand.

Placing and pinning
Follow the envelope instruction sheet for suggested layout plans for your fabric width. These plans are very precise, and, if they are followed correctly, your pattern pieces should fit on perfectly.

Always lay your pattern on a large flat surface; never let the fabric hang over a table edge, because this distorts and stretches it. First, line up any pattern pieces that use the fabric's fold. Accuracy is key, because even a small slither added or subtracted will change the size of your garment.

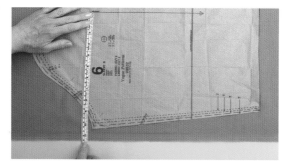

1 Using a tape, measure from the pattern grain line to the selvage at each end of each pattern piece to ensure the grain remains straight.

Tip
• When pinning, keep the pins clear of the cutting line—this will prevent you from blunting your shears!

2 Hold it still with weights; when the position of each piece is checked, you can pin it in place. Place the pins along the seam allowance, perpendicular to the pattern's edge, and pin diagonally at the corners.

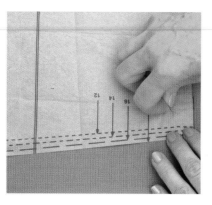

3 Try to place pins so they do not distort the fabric. Distortion can happen if you pin out too much or too little fabric at a time. With special fabrics, such as silk and plastics, where there is the risk of leaving a hole, pin within the seam allowance.

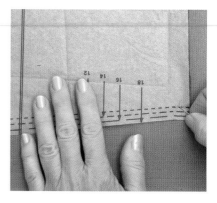

How to mark out your fabric

There are many different methods of marking and transferring details from the pattern to the fabric. It is best to test out the options on your actual fabric before you start.

Some marking methods work better than others on different fabrics. You'll find examples of these on the next three pages. Marking is usually done on the wrong side of fabric. If marking is necessary on the right side, it should be done with basting thread, which can easily be removed.

Choosing your marking method

When marking patterns, how much information is transferred depends on how much sewing experience you have. As a general guide, a novice sewer might need to have all the construction details marked out—whereas an experienced sewer may mark only notches, curved darts, ends of darts, and pocket placements.

There are different types of chalk, pens, and tracing paper that you can use for transferring the markings. As a rule, you should always test the marking method on the fabric first to ensure that it can be removed successfully.

Tailor's chalk or pencils come in different colors, and because of this, they work well on a variety of fabrics. They can usually be removed by brushing out; however, test them before you begin. Chalk can also be used to mark out darts, difficult curved seams, and pocket placements—always mark on the wrong side of the fabric.

Tailor's tacks

Tailor's tacks are a fast and easy way to temporarily mark pocket placements or ends of darts on bulky fabrics, such as thick woolens. The small circles in the images below indicate the position of a dart.

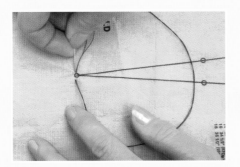

1 Thread a needle with doubled (but not knotted) contrasting thread; locate the mark indicated on the pattern by a small circle.

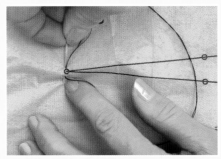

2 Sew through the pattern and two layers of fabric to produce a small stitch.

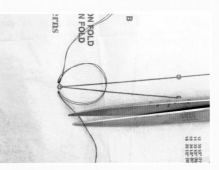

3 With this first stitch, leave a 1in (2.5cm) tail; stitch again through the same spot and leave a 2in (5cm) loop, and then leave another 1in (2.5cm) tail before cutting off. Repeat this process for all the circles marked on the pattern.

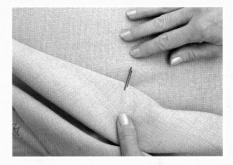

4 Remove all pins from the pattern. Pull the two layers of fabric apart carefully.

5 Snip the threads, leaving an equal amount of thread on both sides.

6 Both sides of the fabric are now marked accurately but temporarily.

Marking with chalk

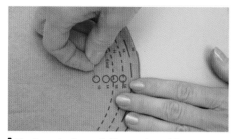

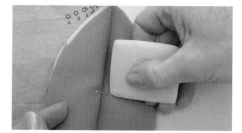

1 Push a pin through the center of the small circle.

2 Pull the two layers of fabric apart.

3 Mark the pin placement with chalk and remove the pin.

Pattern wheel and dressmaker's tracing paper
Test these first on a scrap piece of fabric.

1 Fold your fabric with the wrong sides together. Fold a sheet of tracing paper in half and insert it between the two layers of fabric.

2 Trace the desired line with your tracing wheel.

3 The color comes through, clearly marking the stitching line.

Cutting out
Before cutting out, ensure you have a clean tabletop at a convenient height, keep the fabric flat, and use a sharp pair of shears. Serrated blades are good for knits and slippery fabrics.

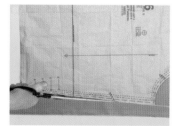

1 Start cutting the pattern out of the fabric as close to the edge of the paper as possible, without cutting the tissue of the pattern. Keep the lower blade of the shears resting on the tabletop as you cut. Try to use long even strokes rather than short choppy ones—this will ensure straighter edges to your pieces.

2 Once the pieces are cut out, you must mark all the notches with small nicks into the seam allowance. Be careful not to cut too far in—⅛in (3 mm) is more than enough to indicate the marks.

Professional tips for cutting out different fabrics

• **Silk and fine fabrics**
When cutting slippery fabrics, always put paper underneath and cut as a single layer. The paper acts as a magnet and helps to keep the fabric still, preventing it from moving away from the scissors as you cut. Serrated scissors are helpful in cutting out silk.

• **Heavy and thick fabrics**
The fabric's thickness may make it necessary and more accurate to cut the pattern out as a single layer.

• **Cutting out a single layer**
Ensure that you cut out all pattern pieces the correct number of times and remember to reverse the pattern for the different sides of the garment.

Sometimes it is useful to use a checklist or to mark the pattern pieces themselves to indicate that you have already cut them out.

Cutting out velvet
Fold the fabric with the pile side out; this will keep the fabric from moving while you cut.

Pocket placement with basting stitch

Machine or hand basting is a temporary way to transfer information from the pattern to the fabric. As the garment is being stitched, you simply remove the basting line. Again, you must test the fabric first to ensure stitching holes or color from the basting thread is not left behind.

When cutting paper patterns in a plaid or print fabric, matching the pockets is necessary. Basting is a fast and easy way to temporarily mark pocket placement.

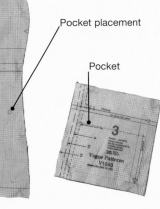

1 Cut out all the main pattern pieces. Cut out the paper pocket pattern.

Pocket placement

Pocket

2 Measure, and then fold under the pocket seam allowance.

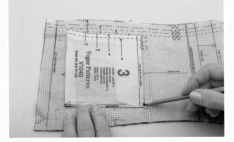

3 Find the small circles indicating the pocket placement, and position the pocket piece on the main pattern.

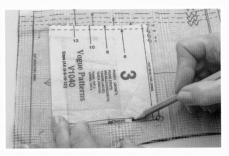

4 With a pencil, mark the prominent fabric design lines on the pocket pattern.

5 Place the pocket pattern onto the fabric and use your pencil lines to match plaids or prints if necessary. Fold out the seam allowance and cut out the pocket.

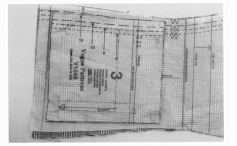

6 Place the pocket pattern, still pinned to the fabric, onto the main pattern to double-check that an accurate fabric match has been made. Then, with a pin, record the pocket placement through both layers of fabric.

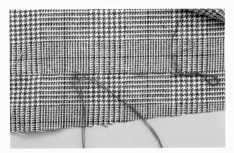

7 Thread a needle with a contrasting thread and, using long stitches, baste the pocket placement position onto the right side of the fabric.

8 Construct the pocket according to the pattern instructions and machine stitch the pocket to the bodice. Try not to catch the basting stitch while sewing, as this can be difficult to remove later. It is possible to remove it as you sew if this becomes a problem.

Altering
a pattern

The following chapter introduces you to some of the easier and more common alterations that you may need to make to your commercial pattern in order to create a custom fit for your garment.

Simple alterations for commercial patterns

All commercial patterns are made to standard average body measurements for each figure type or size.

Companies spend a lot of time and money inviting the public to take part in measurement surveys, eager for their patterns to fit as many people as possible. In reality, of course, we are all different—but standardizing measurements is a necessary process for the industry.

Of course, if your measurements are correct, you are ready for the next step. If not, you will need to customize your pattern to create a more personalized fit—and choosing the correct size will help enormously. It is best to purchase the size that most closely fits your bust and hip measurements. This is because, as a general rule, size alterations are easier to make in other areas.

Creating and altering patterns is a vast subject area with varying degrees of simple and complex methods involved. As a home sewer, you may encounter or have a non-standard body shape (a common reason why people choose to create their own designs).

Certain body shapes require more complex pattern adjustments than the simple adjustments in this following chapter. For example, one requirement might be to adjust the pattern when the bust is disproportionately larger than the chest and other upper body measurements. In this case, enlarging the bust would be easier than altering the other measurements, and the method of adjustment would be more complex—adjustments such as this can be found in a later chapter (see pages 72–79).

Alterations

The alterations to be found in this section are as follows:

- Shortening or lengthening the bodice (see page 50)
- Shortening or lengthening the shoulder (see pages 51–52)
- Altering the bust (see page 52)
- Moving the bust dart up or down (see pages 53–55)
- Increasing the bust by small amounts (see page 55)
- Shortening or lengthening the sleeve (see page 56)
- Shortening or lengthening a skirt (see page 57)
- Increasing or decreasing a skirt waist (see page 57–58)
- Enlarging or reducing a skirt waistband (see page 59)
- Shortening or lengthening a princess-line dress (see page 60)
- Shortening or lengthening pants leg length (see page 61)

Simple rules for pattern alterations

- Always start with flat pressed pattern pieces.

- When making pattern alterations, always pin first and check with a ruler before finally securing down with tape or glue.

- Amending the length of a pattern should be done before all other alterations. Draw a straight line with a long ruler and keep the pattern pieces aligned along it.

- When lengthening, you will need to place tissue paper or pattern tracing paper underneath to fill the gap. Again, pin the new piece into position before securing with tape.

- When shortening pattern pieces, pin them into position and measure again before securing.

- When an alteration has disrupted a seam or dart line, take an average between the two lines, and then smooth and taper a new line.

- When adding or subtracting large amounts (anything over 1in/2.5cm), divide the amount between two or three different places. For example, to add 2in (5cm), slash-and-spread in two places, adding 1in (2.5cm) at each. By distributing the adjustment in this way, you will retain the original design proportion.

- If it is necessary to fold parts of your pattern to reduce its size, remember to take half the measurement required from each side of the tuck, so as not to double the amount. For example, to take out 2in (5cm), take 1in (2.5cm) from the fold to the inside fold and another 1in (2.5cm) from the inside fold to the dotted line.

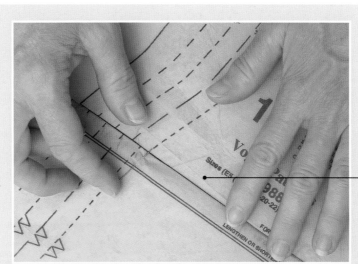

Always pin alterations and re-measure them before securing them permanently.

If you're lengthening a pattern you need to place tissue paper under the pattern to fill the gap.

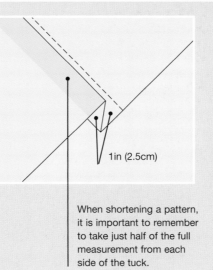

1in (2.5cm)

When shortening a pattern, it is important to remember to take just half of the full measurement from each side of the tuck.

Special note

The patterns used in the following sequences do not include seam allowance. When manipulating your own patterns, keep in mind that a pattern with seam allowance included may look different from these. The basic method of shortening or lengthening a pattern (see page 50) can be applied to all patterns.

Simple bodice alterations
Bodice alterations can affect the armhole and shoulder.

Remember that when making adjustments to any pattern piece, it will affect adjoining pieces. For example, when altering a front bodice, it may affect the back bodice or the sleeves.

Most commercial patterns have a line indicating the best place to shorten or lengthen a pattern. This is a very common alteration and can be done easily. Lengthening or shortening a pattern can disrupt the line of the side seam or dart. Redraw them if necessary, connecting the lines with a ruler or T-square using smooth, tapering lines. If you have a choice, it is always better to increase rather than decrease when drawing.

Lengthening a bodice

1 Locate the "lengthen or shorten" line. Cut along this line as accurately as possible.

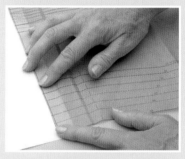

2 Glue some paper to one side of the pattern, keeping the paper flat and neat.

3 From the cut pattern edge, measure the amount to be added, and draw a parallel line. Redraw the grain line onto the new paper with a ruler—this will be used to correctly align the joining pattern piece.

Shortening a bodice

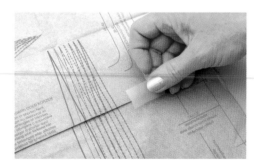

1 Locate all the pattern pieces that you need for your design. Cut them apart from any other pieces, and accurately cut them out in your size.

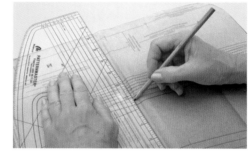

2 Commercial patterns have a printed line on each piece indicating where to shorten and lengthen it. Locate the line, measure the amount to be shortened, and draw a line parallel to the printed line.

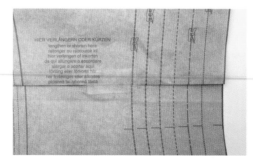

3 Crease the pattern along the printed line and fold down to your pencil line, securing the pattern with tape.

4 Check that the pattern edges are straight and smooth by redrawing them with a ruler and pencil. As a general rule, if a large step is created by making a pattern adjustment, always redraw bigger rather than smaller. Repeat this method for the back bodice.

Shortening the bodice shoulder

The method below shows how to shorten the bodice shoulder while retaining the original garment shape.

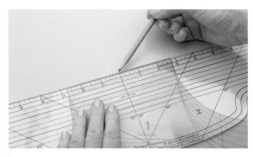

1 Measure to find the center of the shoulder.

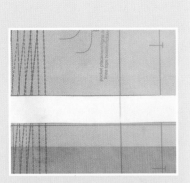

4 Place the joining pattern piece in position, lining it up with the drawn grain line. Be as accurate as possible.

5 Realign the pattern edges, smoothing out any steps and gaps.

6 Repeat this method for the back, using the same measurements.

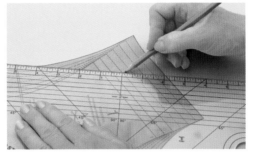

2 With a ruler, connect the center shoulder to a point midway down the armhole, with a straight line that blends into the armhole.

3 Cut along this line from the shoulder to the armhole, leaving a hinge.

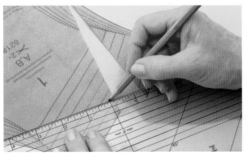

4 Measure in from the line the amount the shoulder is to be shortened by, and mark the pattern with a pencil.

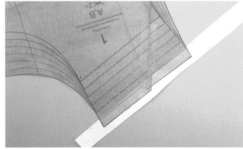

5 Move the hinged shoulder in to meet the pencil mark. Tape the pattern in the correct position, and then glue a strip of paper under the pattern shoulder line.

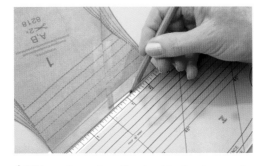

6 With a ruler, redraw the shoulder line to smooth out the step.

7 Repeat this method for the back, using the same measurements.

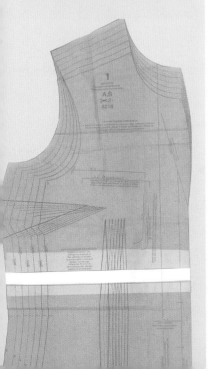

Lengthening the bodice shoulder

The method below shows how to lengthen the bodice shoulder, while retaining the original garment shape.

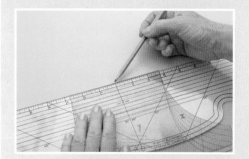

1 Measure to find the center of the shoulder.

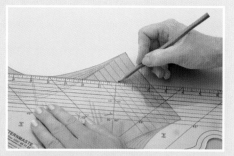

2 With a ruler, connect the center shoulder to midway along the armhole. The straight line should blend into the armhole.

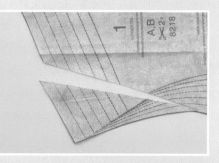

3 Cut along this line from the shoulder to the armhole, leaving a hinge. If you are working with a pattern that includes seam allowance, cut up to the stitch line, and then make a small snip from the pattern paper edge to the stitch line and leave a hinge.

4 Glue a strip of paper to one side of the pattern, measure the amount to be added to lengthen the shoulder, and make a pencil mark.

5 Move the shoulder piece to the measured pencil mark and secure it with tape. Redraw the shoulder line as a smooth, straight line.

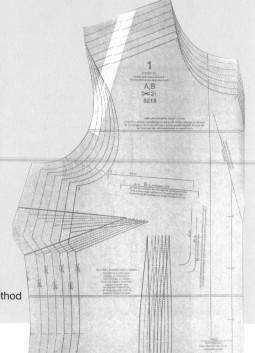

6 The finished pattern piece. Repeat this method for the back

Altering the bust: three methods

Method 1: moving the bust point

Moving the bust point or apex up or down is a quick and simple pattern alteration.

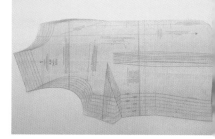

1 First, cut out the front bodice pattern in the correct size.

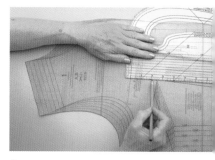

2 With a ruler, draw a line through the center of the side seam dart and the waist dart. The point where the two lines intersect is the bust point or apex.

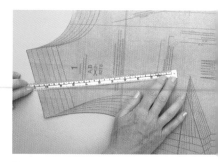

3 Refer to your personalized measurement chart (from page 22) and, on the pattern, measure from the center shoulder down to your own bust point measurement, roughly in line with the pattern's bust point.

4 Once you have your new bust point or apex, connect the new bust point to the side seam dart edges with a ruler.

5 Repeat, connecting the new bust point to the waist dart.

6 To retain the original pattern style and fit, back the new darts away from the new bust point by the same amount as the original pattern indicates.

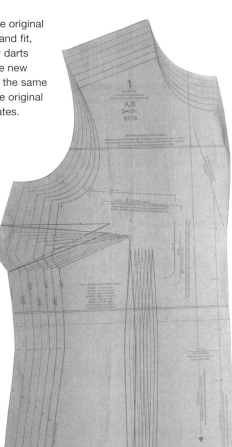

Method 2a: moving the entire bust dart up

This is for adjustments larger than 1in (2.5cm).

1 First cut out the front bodice pattern in the correct size.

2 Draw a box around the bust dart and cut out the bottom and side of the box.

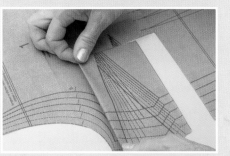

3 Measure the required amount up from the top of the box and mark a parallel line. Crease the top line of the box and fold up to the new line.

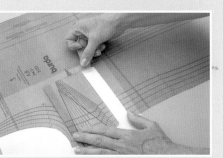

4 Place some paper underneath and tape it in position.

5 With a ruler, realign the side seam and trim any excess paper.

This sequence continues on the next page ➤

6 Fold out the dart and check once again for steps and gaps in the new side seam. It is important to check what implications your alterations may have for the rest of the pattern before cutting it out.

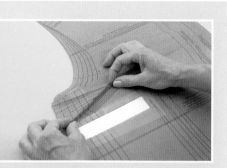

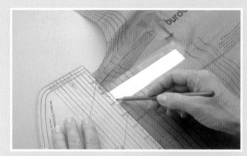

7 With a ruler, redraw the pattern, smoothing out the side seam.

8 With the dart still folded, cut along the new side seam.

9 The finished pattern.

Method 2b: moving the entire bust dart down

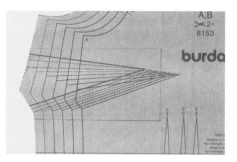

1 Cut out the front bodice pattern in the correct size, draw a box around the bust dart, and then cut out the top and side of the box.

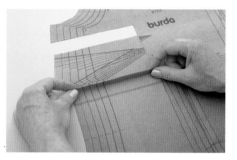

2 Measure the required amount from the bottom of the box, marking a parallel line. Crease the bottom line of the box and fold down to the new line.

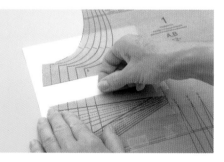

3 Place some paper underneath and tape it in position.

Special note
Remember, the patterns used in these sequences do not have seam allowance.

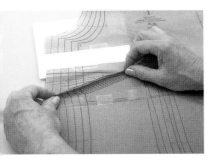

4 Fold out the dart and check for steps and gaps in the new side seam. It is important to check what implications your alterations may have for the rest of the pattern before cutting it out.

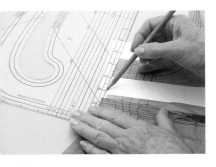

5 With the dart still folded, redraw the side seam, smoothing out any steps and gaps using a ruler.

6 The finished pattern.

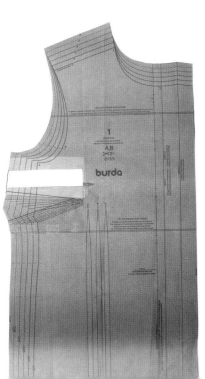

Method 3: increasing the bust by small amounts, ¾in (2cm) or less

When a small amount extra is needed to increase the bust, the seam allowance can be used. Taking too much fabric from the seam allowance will weaken your garment, so small amounts only are possible, i.e., ¾in (2cm) in total. Adding to the bust through the side seams will also add to the armhole circumference. To ensure the sleeve will fit correctly, you will need to add the same amount to the sleeve pattern and to the back.

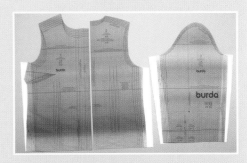

1 Cut out your pattern pieces in the correct size and add extra paper to the side seams of the bodice and sleeve (if there is no seam allowance included on the pattern).

2 Fold out the bust dart.

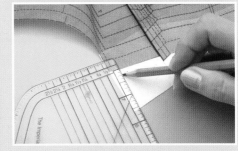

3 Measure out from the side seam the amount to be added (up to ³⁄₁₆in [5mm]).

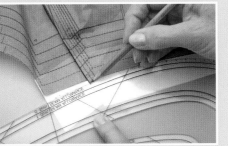

4 With a skirt curve, blend the added measurement into the side seam while the dart is folded closed.

6 Adding to the bust circumference also increases the armhole. Add the same amount to the sleeve biceps width.

5 Keeping the dart folded closed, cut along the new side seam line.

Simple sleeve alterations

How to lengthen or shorten a sleeve.

Lengthening or shortening a sleeve is an easy alteration to do. Simply use the pattern's "shorten or lengthen line" and add or subtract the amount you need.

Lengthening a sleeve

1 Locate the sleeve pattern and cut it out to the required size. Then, locate the printed "shorten or lengthen" line on the pattern and cut along it.

Shortening a sleeve

1 Locate the sleeve pattern and cut it out to the required size. Remember to cut accurately.

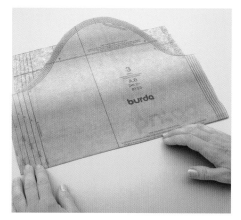

2 Locate the printed "shorten or lengthen" line on the pattern and measure from it the amount to be altered, and draw a parallel pencil line with a ruler. Crease the pattern along the printed line.

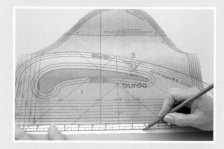

2 Tape or glue some paper to one side of the pattern. With a pencil and ruler, measure out the amount to be added and extend the grain line onto the new paper.

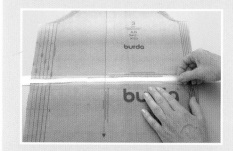

3 Align the other half of the sleeve to the extended grain line and tape it into position.

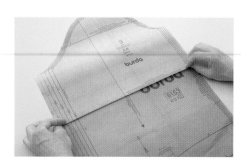

3 Fold down to the measured pencil line and secure the pattern with tape.

Special note
Remember, the patterns used in these sequences do not have seam allowance.

4 Straighten out and redraw the pattern edges with a pencil and ruler.

Simple skirt alterations

Changing the length of a skirt is a quick and simple alteration.

When altering a skirt pattern use the alteration line provided in the same way as for a sleeve. Remember to add or subtract by the same amount on the front and back pieces.

Lengthening or shortening a skirt

1 Locate the skirt pieces, front and back, and cut them out to the required size. Remember to cut accurately.

2 The skirt pattern will include a printed "lengthen and shorten" line. Follow the same step-by-step guide as for lengthening or shortening a sleeve (see page 56).

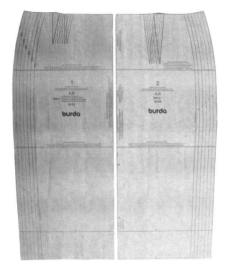

Original skirt pieces

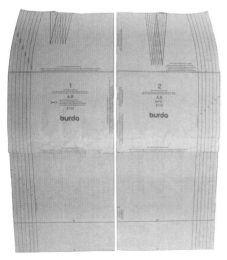

Shortened skirt pieces

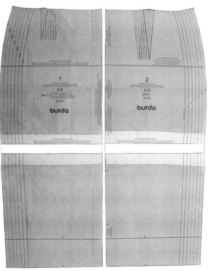

Lengthened skirt pieces

Decreasing a skirt waist

When a skirt fits on the hips and a small alteration is needed to adjust the waist (no more than ¾in/2cm), this method is quick and easy to do.

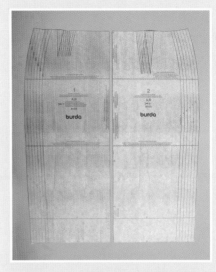

1 Locate the skirt pieces, front and back, and cut them out to the required size. Remember to cut accurately. Divide the total amount needed to change the waist by four. To create a smooth fit, this amount should again be split in two and shared equally between the side seam and the dart.

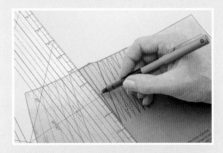

2 Starting with the front skirt, split the measurement again; measure outward, increasing the dart on either side at the waist line. Blend back into the dart end.

This sequence continues on the next page ➤

3 Measure the amount to be reduced at the front waist side seam.

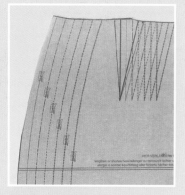

4 With a skirt curve, blend the line back into the side seam.

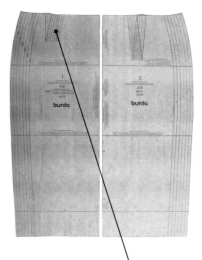

5 Repeat this method, using the same measurements, on the back of the skirt. When both front and back waists have been altered, re-cut the pattern.

Special note
Remember, the patterns used in these sequences do not have seam allowance.

Increasing a skirt waist
When a skirt fits on the hips and a small alteration is needed to adjust the waist (no more than ¾in/2cm), this method is quick and easy to do.

1 Locate the skirt pieces, front and back, and cut them out to the required size. Remember to cut accurately. Divide the total amount needed to change the waist by four. To create a smooth fit, this amount should again be split in two and shared equally between the side seam and the dart.

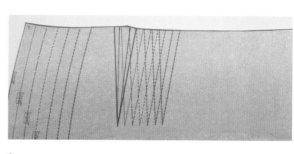

2 Starting with the front skirt, split the measurement again; measure inward, decreasing the dart on either side at the waist line. Blend back into the dart end.

3 In this example, because there is no seam allowance, when cutting larger sizes, you will need to add paper to the side seams. Measure the amount to be added to the waist side seam and blend it back into the hip.

4 Accurately cut the excess paper away.

5 Repeat the method for the back.

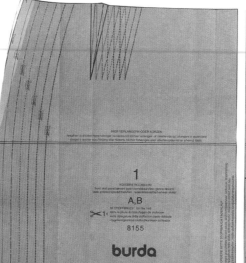

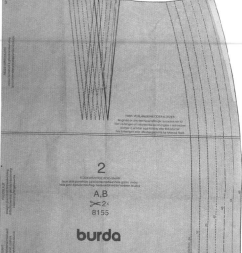

Altering a skirt waistband

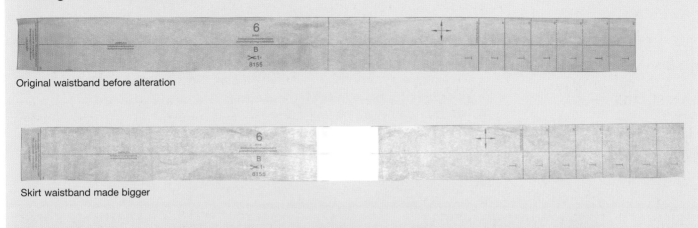

Original waistband before alteration

Skirt waistband made bigger

Skirt waistband made smaller.

Increasing at the hip

To increase through the hip, if no more than ¾in (2cm) is needed.

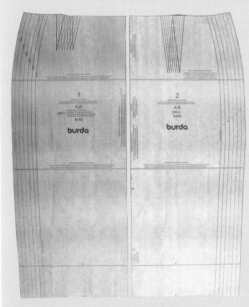

1 Locate the skirt pieces, front and back, and cut them out to the required size. You will also need to alter the hips if you have altered the waistband.

2 Add the amount you need to the hip to make the pattern larger. This will be a quarter of the total amount to be added (2 x fronts, 2 x backs).

3 Blend from the waist line to the new hip measurement and continue down to the hem. Trim away the excess dress sizes.

4 The finished skirt. The extra amount added to the hip should continue down to the hem.

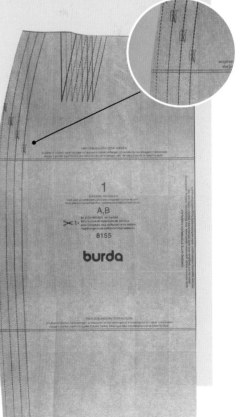

Simple dress alterations
Lengthening or shortening a princess-line dress.

It is especially important to keep the CF and CB lines straight when altering a large pattern such as this princess-line dress. It is important to consider where you need the alteration on the body, as this type of garment covers two alteration points: above and below the waist.

Shortening a princess-line dress
When shortening this pattern, use the CF, CB, or the grain line as a guide to align the pieces. This is important in order to retain the garment's shape.

1 Locate all the pattern pieces required for your design and cut them out to the required size.

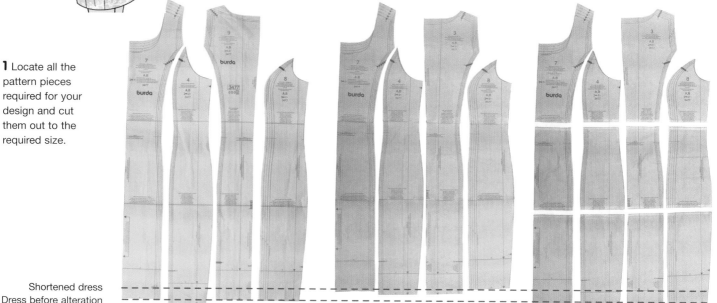

Shortened dress
Dress before alteration
Lengthened dress

2 Measure the amount to shorten the dress by.

3 Draw a parallel pencil line.

4 Make a crease, fold down the required amount, and secure it with tape.

Lengthening a princess-line dress

When lengthening this pattern, use the CF, CB, or the grain line as a guide to align the pieces to. This is important in order to retain the original garment shape.

1 Locate all the pattern pieces required for your design and cut them out to the required size. Locate the desired position for your alteration and cut across the line. Glue or tape on some paper to one half of the pattern and measure out the amount to be added.

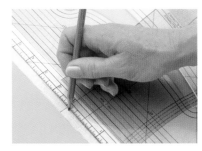

2 Draw a pencil line.

3 Align the other pattern pieces to the grain line, CF, or CB, and secure them with tape. Trim off the excess paper on either side.

Simple pants alterations

This is a simple alteration just for the length of the leg.

Use the lengthen and shorten line as before, remembering to alter the same amount front and back.

Lengthening and shortening pants

When altering pants, align the pattern alterations to the center leg grain line. By doing this, you will retain the original trouser shape.

1 Locate all the pattern pieces required for your design and cut them out. To shorten the pants, follow the same method as for shortening the sleeve (see page 56).

2 When lengthening pants, ensure you line up the grain lines to retain the original trouser style and shape.

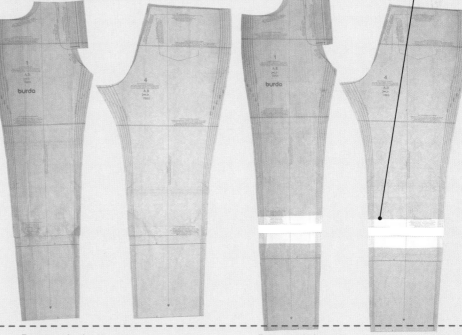

Pants made shorter   Pants made longer

Designing your own patterns

This chapter explores methods for making your own patterns; whether you use the pattern blocks supplied on pages 112–125 of this book, or purchase a ready-made, commercial pattern block from a store. You will learn about making your first toile and altering its fit, as well as how to add design details to the garments that you make.

Creating your own pattern

What is flat pattern cutting?

Flat pattern cutting is a well-established, formulaic, two-dimensional approach to creating and developing paper patterns based on an accurately fitted block. Paper copies of the blocks are then developed and manipulated flat on a tabletop. Three-dimensional shapes are formed by adding in and folding out excess paper to a prescribed formula. A successful final pattern is dependent on how well the block fits the body, the accuracy of the work, the success of the methods used, and how creatively the design has been interpreted by the pattern cutter.

Getting started

This chapter discusses the use of personal blocks as a method for making your own patterns, and how industry uses "working patterns" and "seasonal shapes" to speed up the design process. There are several different ways to create block patterns; only two are covered in detail in this book. In the first, scaled-down blocks are resized using a grid system—these blocks are supplied on pages 112–125 with instructions on how to scale them up to full size on page 66. The second method is to buy a ready-made commercial pattern block from a store.

You will learn about making your first toile—a fabric prototype of the garment you are making—and assessing and altering its fit (see page 68). Once the blocks have been perfected, you're ready for the more creative practice of designing your own garments. For this you need to understand design analysis, looking closely at the initial design sketch and interpreting its construction details into a clear "working drawing." Marking out a dress form with yarn to the correct proportions, from the position of seam lines to the width of the button stand is an easy way to visualize the information before transferring it to a paper pattern (see page 80).

What is a basic block?

A basic block is the original drafted pattern that has been perfected to fit the body precisely. Once this pattern has been tested for fit, it becomes the base that all other patterns are derived from. This original block should never be cut up for manipulations, and it should be altered only if your body shape changes. It never includes a seam allowance; this makes pattern manipulation more accurate. To make it easier to trace around and to prolong its life, the finished pattern block can be traced onto cardstock.

This simple, basic pattern will fit the body with just enough ease for freedom of movement (see page 31). Any design shaping, flare, or detailing is created at the next stage. A half toile of the pattern is often sufficient to assess the fit; however, a full garment may be necessary if the right side of the body is different from the left. It takes time and patience to perfect the shape and it is not uncommon to make two or more toiles to get it right. Remember, you will need to add seam allowance to the pattern in order to sew the toile together.

What is a seasonal shape?

A "seasonal shape" involves more design input than a working pattern and is therefore the next stage in the process. A seasonal shape in the fashion industry is one that is going to be repeated throughout that season's collection—once perfected, it will also benefit from being copied to cardstock for continued reuse. Examples would include a blouse with shoulder pads or a lowered waistline on a pair of jeans. The pattern cutter would start with the basic block and adapt its detailing to the design's specifications. Thereafter, all the blouses and jeans in that collection could be cut from this block, avoiding the need to start at the beginning each time.

Calculating fabric requirements

When designing your own patterns, you'll need to know how much fabric to buy. To do this, cut out the pattern pieces and, bearing in mind the grain direction and fold lines, lay out the pieces on any spare lengths of 36in (90cm) and 56in (140cm) wide fabric. This physical positioning of pieces makes it easier to see if two pieces will fit side by side and how much room there is to spare. Do not forget to allow for a seam allowance, and remember to allow extra fabric if the fabric chosen has a strong pattern that needs to be aligned across a seam (see pages 37–40).

Methods for creating basic blocks

There are several ways to create your own personal pattern blocks—two are covered in this book. The method you choose is merely a question of personal preference. The basic block consists of five simple pieces: a darted bodice front and back, a sleeve, and a skirt front and back. The skirt and bodice can be joined to make a dress.

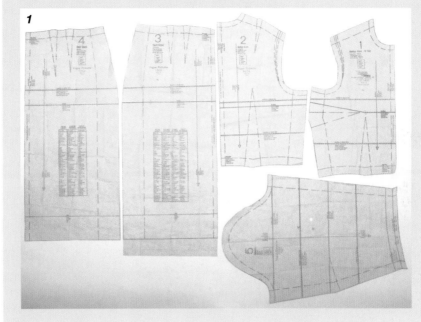

Working pattern: raglan sleeve

A working pattern is made from a basic block but is one stage farther on in the design, such as a raglan sleeve, where the bodice and sleeve patterns have been permanently joined to make a new shape, a kimono sleeve, or a basic T-shirt. These accurate working patterns, once toiled and perfected, can also be transferred to cardstock and kept for future use.

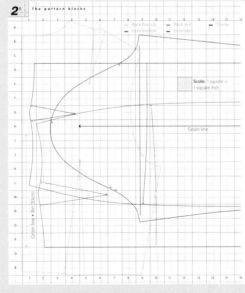

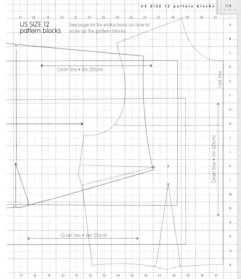

1 The commercial block pattern or fitting shell

This is a store-bought pattern that you can purchase in standard sizes and alter to fit. Instructions are provided for making personal alterations.

2 Using pattern blocks

Use the blocks provided on pages 112–125. Follow the step-by-step guide on page 66 for resizing the pattern blocks onto grid paper.

Using pattern blocks

How to create a custom-made pattern using basic blocks.

It is possible to create unique patterns using basic handmade or commercial block patterns and your own body measurements. Your custom-made blocks can be mounted onto cardstock and used again and again to create new patterns.

How to scale up pattern blocks

On pages 112–125, you can find scaled-down pattern blocks in seven sizes. You can use these to make your own personal blocks. To make enlarging the patterns easier, each column and row is identified with a letter or number. Each square on the grid represents a 1in (2.5cm) square on your pattern tracing paper or graph paper. See below for the scaling-up method.

How to use a commercial block pattern

Most companies that produce commercial patterns also produce a commercial block (or "sloper") in various sizes. They feature in the same pattern catalog books as regular patterns, and can be purchased in department stores and fabric shops.

Commercial block patterns are very convenient to use, saving a lot of the time that is involved in drafting your own. Block patterns are arranged in one size per envelope, so you will need to know the size you require before you buy one. (For advice on sizing, see page 22.)

Commercial block patterns are the master patterns that all other patterns are based on. For ease of use, these block patterns are produced with large seam allowances so that alterations can

Scaling up the blocks

Before you start, you will need to either draft your own grid paper, download it from the Internet and paste it together as letter (A4) size sheets, or buy dressmakers' pattern paper with 1in (2.5cm) squares. If you are drafting your own grid paper, it is important to keep checking your measurements, ensuring that all the lines are parallel.

The blocks do not include seam allowance. Once you have enlarged the patterns you will need to add seam allowance before making up the toile. Seam allowance is ⅝in (1.5cm).

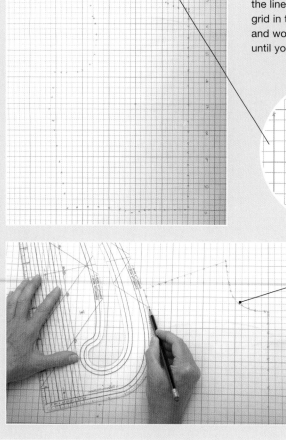

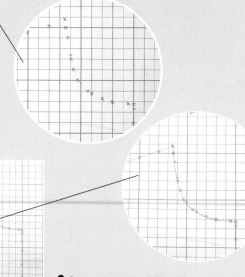

1 On your grid paper, start by labeling all the 1in (2.5cm) columns with letters, and the rows with numbers. Each 1in (2.5cm) square on your grid paper is represented by one grid square in the book. Mark out a small "X" on your grid where the lines in the diagrams are positioned on the grid in the book. Start at the top left-hand corner and work your way around the pattern clockwise until you can see the outline of the pattern.

2 Connect up the "X"s with a ruler and a skirt curve.

be made easily and any changes recorded straight onto the pattern. Often commercial patterns suggest a fabric, such as gingham or plaid, so that the toile's balance can be easily assessed using the vertical and horizontal lines.

Inside the envelope are detailed instructions on how to take accurate body measurements, how to make adjustments to the fit of the first toile, and even advice on design suitability for different body shapes.

Commercial blocks
Commercial suppliers, such as Vogue, sell block patterns that take a lot of the work out of making your own.

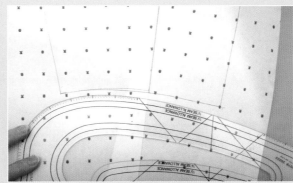

3 When you have finished connecting the "X"s, using a skirt curve, trace off the finished shape onto a fresh sheet of pattern tracing paper.

4 Fold out the darts to make sure they line up and match. This is a good way to ensure that the same curve or straight line is continued from one side of the dart to the other. Even out any lumps and bumps.

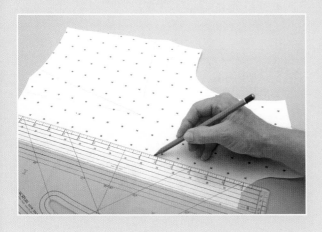

5 Before cutting out, measure the pattern pieces to ensure that they are correct. For example, check that the front and back side seams of a skirt are the same length. Cut out, and then label, name, and mark all the pattern pieces with grain lines, notches, and so on.

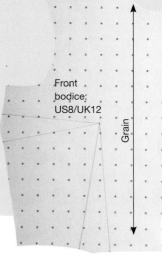

Front bodice: US8/UK12

Grain

Making and fitting a toile

Make a toile to test the fit of the garment you're creating.

Having checked the accuracy of your block, you are now ready to make your first toile. A toile is an early version of a garment made in inexpensive fabric to test a pattern—a kind of fabric prototype. You may make multiple toiles during the process of perfecting your block.

Preparation

First, you need to press the creases from some medium-weight muslin with a steam iron. Fold the muslin in half with the grain. Trace off your blocks onto a new sheet of pattern tracing paper and add seam allowance. Place the pattern pieces on the muslin parallel to the grain line, and trace around them with a pencil. Mark on the CF and CB, and draw in the bust lines, waist lines, the biceps line, and the elbow line. Mark in the hip line on the skirt and all the grain lines. It is important to mark these out on the muslin so that once you have made up the garment, you can see if the lines are balanced and in alignment with the body.

Sewing your toile together

Sew your toile together with seam allowance of ⅝in (1.5cm); ensure that you are accurate throughout or you will alter the size of your toile. Sew the darts first while the pieces are flat. Press the front darts toward the CF and the back darts toward the CB. Next, sew the front and back bodice shoulder seams and side seams together and press them open. Sew up the underarms of both sleeves and then set the sleeves into the finished armholes (see page 134). Do not press the sleeve caps or you will flatten out the ease. For the skirt, make the darts first before sewing up the side seams.

Methodical working

When you are pattern cutting, it is good practice to work in a methodical manner. Create a history of how your pattern was drafted and all the stages that this involves. When a mistake becomes apparent, it is then easier to retrace your steps and identify where the mistake happened. Many mistakes are made through adding seam allowances to some pattern pieces and not to others, or sewing pieces together the wrong way up. Working in a step-by-step way helps to keep mistakes and inaccuracies to a minimum. Never be tempted to ignore a problem. Chopping pieces off your patterns or toiles will usually show up on the finished article. So sorting out problems at the paper pattern stage will save valuable time and money.

Tips for working methodically

Working methodically allows you more scope to be creative once you have learned the basic principles.

- Trace your blocks onto cardstock to differentiate them from your patterns.

- Label everything thoroughly, with the name and date of the block or pattern piece i.e., Left Skirt Front (cut 1), Cuff (cut 4), Cut on Fold, and so on. Mark on the CB and CF lines, grain lines, balance lines, notches and size of seam allowance. This will help to avoid confusion at every stage.

- Trace off the pattern pieces at every stage of pattern manipulation, and keep and label the stages. Only when you have finished your flat pattern manipulations, and you are ready to try out your toile, should you put the seam allowance on the pattern.

- Always put the seam allowance on the final pattern.

- Always write on your pieces the right way up and on the correct side—if necessary mark "Right Side Up" (RSU) on pieces that can't be turned over.

- Notches are vital for matching up pattern pieces, for checking them at the pattern stage, and for sewing up—don't forget to put them on, as it will save you a great deal of time later (see page 83).

- Cut one pattern piece at a time, and check all the pattern pieces to ensure that they fit together where necessary.

- Mark on all the darts and details on your fabric pieces with tailor's tacks or chalk (see page 43).

- When sewing your toile together, always sew to the seam allowances you have put on your pattern. If you are inaccurate by even a fraction of an inch, the size of your toile will be altered considerably.

- Any alterations that you make on your toile should be copied to your pattern immediately, before you forget what or where they were. Don't forget to add seam allowances back on where you have chopped parts off your pattern.

Try on your toile

Before trying on your toile for the first time, tie some elastic around your waist—this will mark the natural waistline—and mark the fullest part of the bust and low hip on your undergarments or a leotard with sticky tape to check that these points on your body line up with the relevant points on your toile.

Using a dress form

If you have invested in a dress form, you could fit your toile to a dress form padded out to your own personal measurements (see page 80).

What is balance in a garment?

Perfect balance is when a garment's CF, CB, waist line, and hip lines are aligned with the corresponding points on the body. It is important to balance your toile correctly, because all other garments will be produced from this base. Getting this right will remove the need to correct all subsequent garments that you produce using this block.

Perfect figure,
balanced garment

Imperfect figure
unbalanced garment

Imperfect figure
balanced garment

Tip

• To find the true CF, make a plumb line by tying a string loosely around your neck. Thread another length of string loosely through it and tie a slightly weighted object on the end. Arrange the plumb line at the CF neck and let it hang down. Mark the exact CF line with sticky tape on your undergarments or leotard, and repeat the process for the CB.

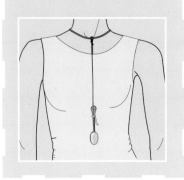

Assessing the fit of your toile

When you try on your toile for the first time, stand back and look at your garment in a long mirror. Assess the fit and notice the position of the balance lines on the toile. Check that the CF, CB, waist, bust, and hip lines align to your own body. It is important to stand straight and look forward. Ask someone to help you with this stage, as it can be difficult, particularly when trying to see the back. Looking down or twisting will render the assessment of fit inaccurate.

Be aware of how the garment feels on the body—the bodice should be fitted, but not tight. Notice any excess loose fabric or pulling across the garment. The armhole must not feel restricted, and you should be able to move your arm freely. Remember to look at the side seams and check that they are on your sides and not drifting forward or backward.

Taking your time to properly assess and alter the toile at this stage will be worthwhile. A perfectly fitted block will ensure that the designs you produce subsequently will fit you beautifully.

1 Tie a cord or length of elastic around your natural waist. Compare the tied line to the waist line marked on the toile. If, as shown here, the two lines are not the same, the waist line will need to be adjusted on the pattern.

Making simple toile adjustments

If the toile is too big:
Pinch out any obvious excess fabric through the seams and darts of your toile, making sure that the balance lines remain straight. Mark the adjustments with a pencil, and transfer them to your pattern.

If the toile is too small:
Unpick the restricted area, releasing the tension. Measure the gap that is created, and add in the amounts needed where necessary.

Fitting the sleeve

You can assess the sleeve fit when it is on the stand or on the body. The center grain running down the sleeve should line up slightly in front of the skirt or trouser side seam. Look at the sleeve on the arm to see that the wrist is central within the sleeve hem, and check that the sleeve is not dragging up against the arm at the front or back. If dragging is present, take the sleeve out and readjust the sleeve cap by moving it around the armhole either forward or backward. This may be only a very slight adjustment, no more than ¼in (6mm).

Incorrect sleeve alignment
This alignment would cause the sleeve to drift toward the back.

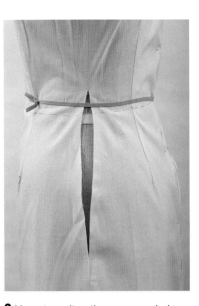

Making major toile adjustments

You will need to permanently alter your toile if any adjustments are major, and perhaps even make another. Always ensure you make the corresponding adjustments to your pattern. Toiling is an important part of making your own patterns, and often several are needed before the fit is completely right.

2 Here, two alterations are needed. The bodice is too long and the waist is too small. To correct this, measure the difference between the elastic and the pencil line; this will give you the amount to shorten the bodice pattern by. The tightness at the waist is best adjusted by opening the side seams. Measure the amount of extra room required and add it to the pattern.

Correct sleeve alignment
The central sleeve grain should start ⅜in (1cm) behind the bodice shoulder line. The biceps line should be horizontal and the central grain should continue down slightly in front of the garment side seam.

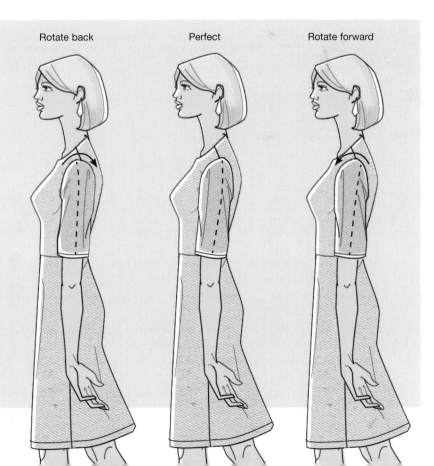

Rotate back   Perfect   Rotate forward

Advanced pattern alterations

To perfect the fit of your pattern, you may need to make some alterations.

Whether you have used the blocks on pages 112–125 or purchased a commercial pattern block, it is likely you will have to make some alterations to the fit. Having checked the balance of your garment and assessed how it feels on the body, you will have some idea of the areas on the garment that may need attention. You will already have taken out or added in any simple alterations (see page 48). The following pages focus on some of the more specialized alterations you may need to make to your pattern to perfect your toile.

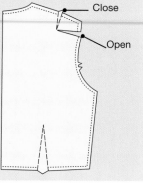

Fitting the bodice

When fitting the bodice, it is important to consider how one alteration affects the rest of the bodice.

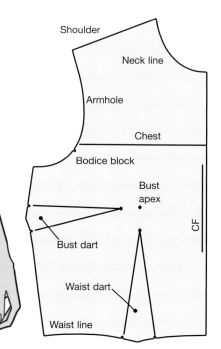

Shoulder
Neck line
Armhole
Chest
Bodice block
Bust apex
Bust dart
Waist dart
Waist line
CF

Decreasing and increasing the bodice armholes.

If you have a sleeveless dress and the armhole gapes or pinches the body, the following pattern alterations will correct this. Likewise, if your garment sleeves are baggy or if you find the armhole binds and pinches the body, these alterations will work. Remember that these alterations will have a direct effect on the sleeve. So when increasing or decreasing the armhole you will also need to adjust the sleeve (see page 56).

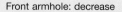
Front armhole: decrease

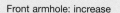
Front armhole: increase

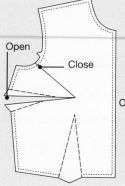
Open
Close

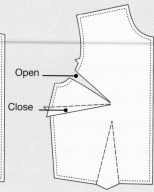
Open
Close

Back armhole: decrease
Open
Close

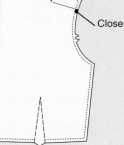
Back armhole: increase
Close
Open

Fitting and adjusting the armhole

A smooth, nicely fitted armhole is essential for comfort and when setting in a sleeve. Having tried on your garment, be aware of any pulling or tightness. Look to see if there is excessive fullness in the front or back of the armhole.

The armhole alterations shown here may be necessary if you notice any excess fabric. Remember, if you take fabric out of the armhole in this way, it will affect the sleeve. If you are having problems with a sleeve, removing the sleeve and looking at how the armhole fits often helps.

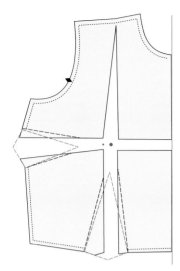

Increasing the bust

This alteration allows you to change the bust measurements without affecting the rest of the bodice. This alteration should be done only if there is a discrepancy of 2in (5cm) between the chest measurement and the bust measurement, or if you are a size C cup or larger.

Slash the bodice block from the center shoulder point through the bust apex and down to the waist, and horizontally from the CF, through the bust apex to the side seam. The amount to add depends on the individual.

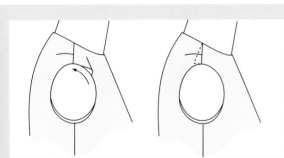

Front
Correction of fullness in the front of the armhole.

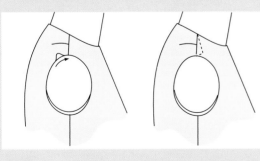

Back
Correction of fullness in the back of the armhole.

Adjusting the sleeve after lowering the bodice armhole

If your bodice armhole is too tight, you may need to lower it. This will affect your sleeve. The following sequence explains how to do this.

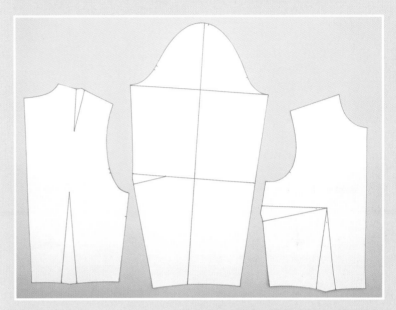

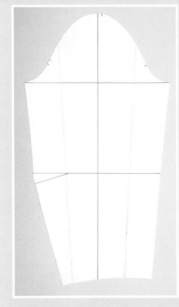

1 Trace off the bodice and sleeve blocks and cut them out.

2 Divide the sleeve into equal lengthwise quarters.

3 Measure down 1in (2.5cm) on the sleeve underarm seam.

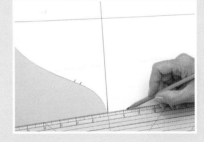

4 Using the marks you've just made, draw and blend a curved line to the first quarter point on the front and back sleeve cap, creating a new armhole shape. Cut away the excess paper.

This sequence continues on the next page ➤

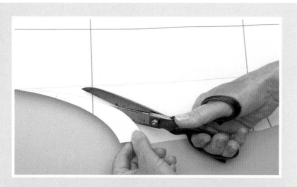

5 On the sleeve only this time, measure down 1in (2.5cm) at the underarm and again draw in a smooth curve to the first quarter point at the sleeve cap. Cut along this line, but not all the way through; keep a hinge at the sleeve cap.

6 Using the hinge, pivot each section the same amount as you originally lowered the armhole. This alteration will add width at the biceps for movement, while retaining the larger armhole size.

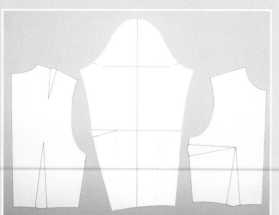

7 Place paper underneath and secure the pivots with tape or glue, and cut out the new shape. To complete the pattern, lower the bodice armhole at the side seam by 1in (2.5cm) and gently shape into the armhole as you did with the sleeve. Transfer the armhole notches front and back, keeping to roughly the same position.

Fitting the sleeve

Basic sleeve fit

A basic sleeve should fit into the armhole smoothly. The center grain should align slightly forward of the garment side seam when hanging loosely down. The biceps line should be at a 90-degree angle to this grain line.

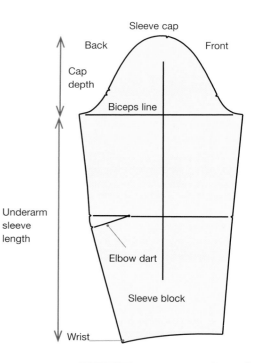

Sleeve cap

Back   Front

Cap depth

Biceps line

Underarm sleeve length

Elbow dart

Sleeve block

Wrist

Increasing and reducing cap ease

Almost all sleeves have ease in the "cap" or sleeve head. This helps with movement and gives the sleeve shape. When making up a master pattern or personal block, there should be a minimum ⅜in (1cm) of ease in the back sleeve and ¼in (0.5cm) in the front.

The amount of ease can vary with the type of fabric used (see page 31). Leather and plastics are difficult to manipulate into an armhole. If you are working with fabrics such as these, you will need to reduce the cap ease.

If you find there is too much or too little ease in your sleeve cap, follow the simple "slash and spread" method, right.

1 Trace off the sleeve block and cut out. Cut down the center line on the sleeve cap to the biceps line and then out to each side seam, retaining paper hinges.

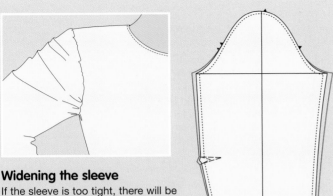

Widening the sleeve

If the sleeve is too tight, there will be no movement in your sleeve. If, when reaching upward, the whole garment pulls up, you may need to add width to the biceps of your sleeve.

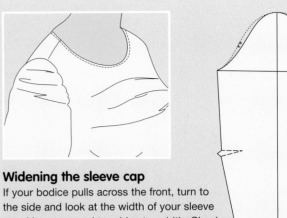

Widening the sleeve cap

If your bodice pulls across the front, turn to the side and look at the width of your sleeve cap. You may need to add extra width. Check by unpicking the armholes in the front and back to release the tightness. This is the amount you will need to add to your pattern.

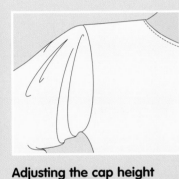

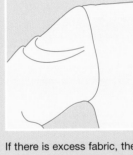

Adjusting the cap height

If your sleeve pulls from the top of the sleeve cap, then you may need to lengthen the cap.

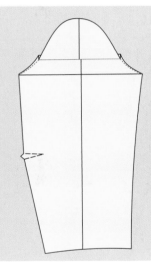

If there is excess fabric, then you may need to shorten the cap.

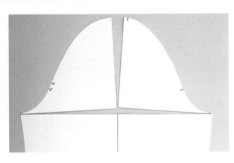

2 To increase the sleeve cap ease, pivot out the pattern pieces from the hinges.

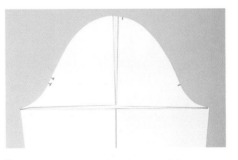

3 Place paper behind and secure it in position with glue or tape. Smooth out any lumps and bumps by re-drawing the line.

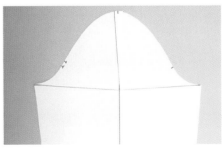

4 To decrease the sleeve cap, overlap the pattern pieces by the required amount using the hinged pieces, and secure it in position. Attach to the paper and smooth out any lumps and bumps.

Fitting skirts

To achieve a well-fitted skirt, first try the skirt on and assess the fit. Note any excess fabric, if the balance lines are straight across the hip, and if they are straight down the CF, CB, and side seams. If the skirt feels too tight across the front or back, the following alteration is a quick fix.

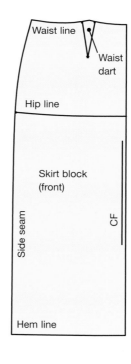

Waist line

Waist dart

Hip line

Skirt block (front)

Side seam

CF

Hem line

Adding in extra room for rounded figure shapes

If the side seam is pulling to the back or front, this is an indication that more room is needed over the stomach or backside. The method shown here is for creating more room in one area, while leaving the rest of the garment alone. This puts the extra room exactly where it is needed.

Taking out extra fullness across the skirt back

If there is excess fabric across the hollow of the back of the skirt, you can remove it as shown below. The excess can be pinned out from the side seam toward the CB seam and then taken out of the pattern as a wedge.

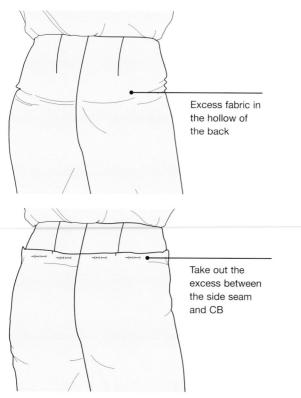

Excess fabric in the hollow of the back

Take out the excess between the side seam and CB

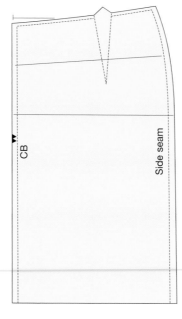

CB

Side seam

Adjust the pattern

Slash the pattern from the CB to the side seam, leaving a hinge. Redraw the CB line in straight, ensuring that you maintain a 90-degree angle at the top.

Too tight across the back

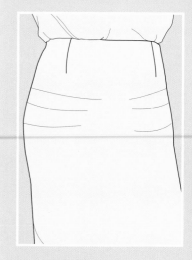

Too tight across the front

2 Cut down from waist to hem, keeping a hinge at the hem. Cut from the CF or CB hip line to the side seam, keeping a hinge at the side seam.

3 Spread the pattern by the required amount. This alteration increases the dart width and lengthens the CF or CB, without changing the hem or the length of the side seam.

4 Glue or tape paper underneath.

1 Trace off the front and back skirt blocks and cut out. Divide the skirt block in half at the hip line and draw a line from waist to hem.

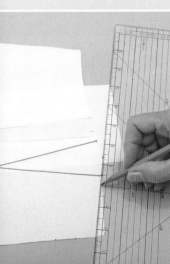

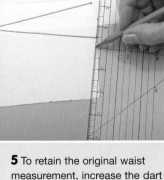

7 Smooth out the side seams and CF or CB. When doing this, it is better to add to the pattern than to take away.

5 To retain the original waist measurement, increase the dart by the amount added.

6 Blend in the waist shaping, smoothing out any lumps and bumps.

Fitting pants

To achieve a well-fitted pair of pants it is important to understand how pants fit. The way the upper body of the pair of pants fits will dictate how the rest behaves. The two most important measurements are the crotch depth (this measurement is taken while sitting down; measure from waist to chair seat at the side seam) and crotch length (the measurement from CF to CB between the legs). (See also pages 22–23, Body landmarks.)

If your pants are too tight or too loose around the crotch, you may need to alter the crotch depth. Compare your crotch depth measurement with the pattern. If you need to make an alteration, make sure you shorten or lengthen the same amount front and back. If you need to make alterations to both the crotch depth and crotch length, you must change the crotch depth first. It is always good practice to add or subtract exactly where you need to on the pattern.

Waist line
Crotch length
Waist dart
Crotch depth
Crotch line
Pants block (front)
CF
Knee line
Side seam
Hem line

Shortening crotch depth and leg length

1 Take your front and back pants blocks or patterns and cut out. From the hip line, measure the amount the pattern is to be shortened by and draw a parallel pencil line.

2 Crease along the hip line and fold up to the measured pencil line. Tape in place and repeat the process for the back.

3 This process shortens the total length of the pants.

Adding extra room for a rounded stomach or backside

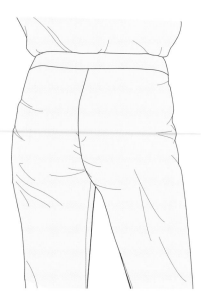

Increasing crotch length

If the measurement is still too long or short after changing the crotch depth, you may need to alter the crotch length.

A close-fitting or relaxed pants fit will determine the amount of ease needed. This could be anything from ⅝in (1.3cm) to 1½in (3.8cm) in length, depending on the pants style.

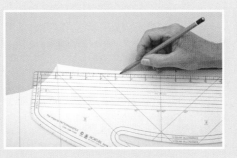

1 Draw a line from the curve of the CF crotch straight down to the inside leg.

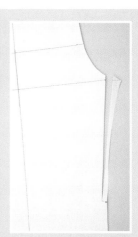

2 Cut along this line down to the inside leg. Do not cut through, leave a hinge. Pivot the piece outward, increasing the crotch length by the desired amount using the hinge. Add some paper underneath.

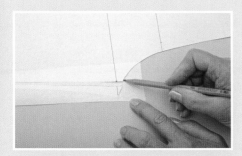

3 Redraw, smoothing out the new crotch line. Repeat the same method for the back crotch seam. If you need to add any more than 1in (2.5cm) to the crotch length, this should be added above the waist line.

4 If your pants are still too short through the crotch after adding to the depth and length, you may need to add at the CF and CB waist as well. Add paper to the CF and CB patterns at the waist.

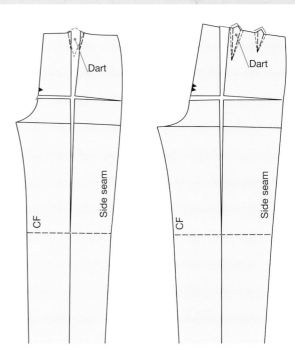

5 Measure up from the waist line at the CF and CB and draw a curve, continuing the seam line upward, then blend back into the waist line. Trim off the excess paper.

Method 1

If your pants are too tight across the backside, an easy method by which to loosen them is to add extra to the pattern side seam.

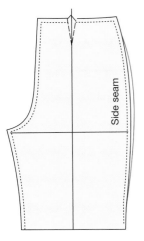

Method 2

Slash down the grain line to the knee and out to the side seams. Do not cut through at the knee; keep a paper hinge. Next, cut horizontally from the CB or CF to the side seam, again being careful not to cut through. Add or subtract exactly where you need it. Keep the pattern straight, adding equal amounts. If you need to keep the original waist measurement, take in the extra by enlarging the darts. When you are finished, smooth out by redrawing the seams. Make the opposite pattern adjustment for a flat stomach or backside.

Designing patterns

Now that you have perfected your basic blocks, you are ready to attempt your first designs.

To realize your design ideas, it helps to understand proportion and where seam lines look most flattering on the body.

Using yarn or tape to map out style lines on a dress form is a good way to see your design three-dimensionally. On the following pages, a standard US size 6 (UK size 8) dress form is used. If you are not of a standard size, you may need to adapt a dress form to suit your own personal measurements.

Design analysis

Designers often put their inspirations onto paper. The designer's sketch is this initial idea. It is an interpretation of how a garment is to look when it is finished. It shows how the fabric will behave, may include color and texture, and will evoke the general feeling of the garment.

Working drawing

One of the first steps in realizing your design is to make a working drawing. A working drawing is a simple line drawing of the garment that highlights the details of its construction—where to put the seam lines, darts, gathers or pleats, topstitching, buttonholes, and so on. Based on the designer's sketch, the working drawing should be in proportion, with the lines drawn exactly where you wish them to appear on the body. Drawing the design like this helps you to focus and consider these details, which are paramount at this stage, as they will inform how the pattern will be cut.

Details to consider

Before starting to construct the pattern you should have an idea of what fabric the garment is to be made in. The blouse shown at right is to be made from a woven cotton shirting fabric and is therefore not stretchy. (Woven fabric can sometimes contain a small amount of stretch. The amount of stretch is an important consideration when choosing a fabric, as the pattern will have to be adapted for this.) The fit of this garment is achieved through four darts with gathering at the front and back yoke. The

Padding out a dress form to your own size

In the fashion industry, a common method for fitting garments to individual sizes is to pad out a solid, linen-covered dress form in a small size to fit your own measurements. In this way, it is possible to completely recreate your own body shape.

You will need
- Dress form smaller than your own body size
- Pins
- Tape measure
- Scissors
- Batting
- Padded bra in your size
- Elastic
- Strong jersey fabric

Using the measurement chart on page 22, compare your own measurements to those of the dress form, starting at the top and working down, use batting to pad out the dress form to match your size. Once the dress form is padded, you can pin elastic or yarn onto the stand to indicate where the new hip and bust lines will be.

Put the padded bra onto the stand and stuff the cups with batting. Measure to ensure you are creating the correct bust size.

Pin a layer of stretch jersey over the whole form to create a smooth surface to work on.

Pad the waist with strips of batting. Start with narrow strips, layering up the batting, and using wider strips each time. Measure the waist to check the proportions.

yoke does not have a natural shoulder line seam. The neckline is round and slightly dropped at the CF neck.

Details such as the size of the button are essential at this stage, as this informs the width of the button stand—one of the first steps in cutting this pattern. Follow the step-by-step instructions below to translate your working drawing into a pattern.

Translating a working drawing into a pattern

Pinning the style lines on the dress stand can help you to see the proportions of the garment on the body more clearly. Basic blocks are flat representations of a dress stand or form. In these images, the model is a standard size 6 (UK size 8). Visualizing the proportions in this way means you can measure the distances accurately and transfer them straight onto the pattern paper.

You will need
- Working drawing
- Dress stand
- Yarn
- Pins
- Pattern tracing paper
- Red pen
- Pencil

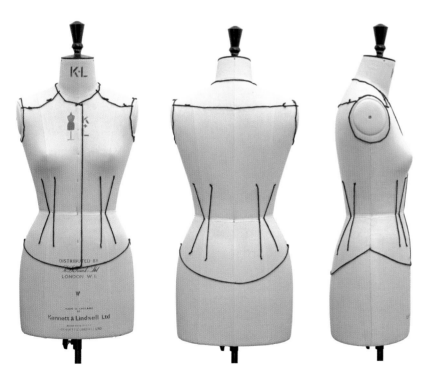

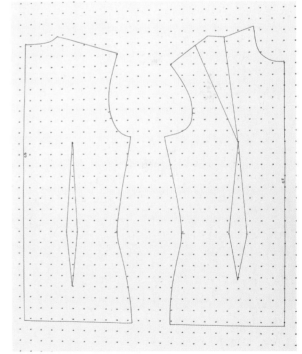

1 From your working drawing, map out the style lines on the dress stand using yarn and pins, front and back. Always stand back from the dress form to look at and assess the proportion and accuracy of the design.

2 Trace off the appropriate block for the design onto pattern tracing paper—in this case a torso block (see page 96). You will use this flat block in correspondence with the dress form—ensure they are both the same size. Trace in red pen to indicate the original block pattern.

This sequence continues on the next page ➤

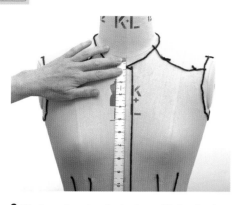

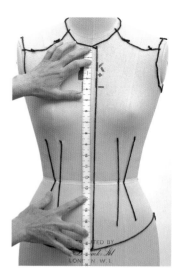

3 Work on the stand, starting with the front neckline. Measure the distance between the CF stand neckline and your own CF yarn neckline.

4 With a pencil, mark the yarn line onto the pattern tracing paper. Continue measuring and marking the relevant positions on the pattern paper.

5 Measure from the CF yarn neckline to the design's hem.

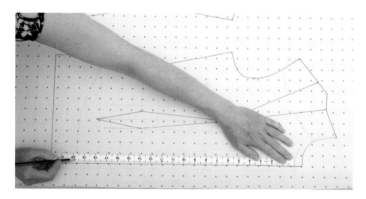

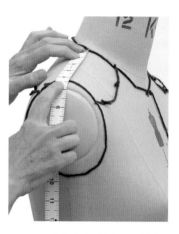

7 Work systematically from the top front of the stand to the top back of the stand, transferring the design to the pattern tracing paper. Use the stand's shoulder seams, waist line seam, and side seams as reference points in relation to the block shoulder seams, waist seam, and side seams.

6 Transfer the measurements to the pattern tracing paper.

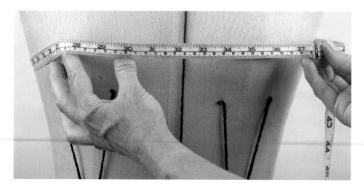

8 Decide on the garment's fit—tight, loose, etc. (see page 32). If the fit you want to achieve around the body is larger than the block bust, take the tape measure and place it around the bust. You must now judge how large you would like your design to be. Measure the bust on your block and compare the difference. Take that difference and divide it by four, and add the same amount to each side seam level with the bust.

9 The block pattern has one dart and our design has two darts. To split one dart into two, find the center of the block dart and draw two vertical lines equidistant from it. Measure the dart and split the measurement of the dart equally between the two. Redraw the darts to the same length as before.

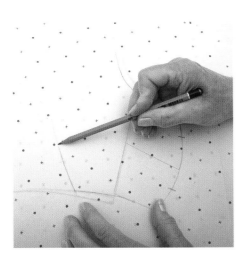

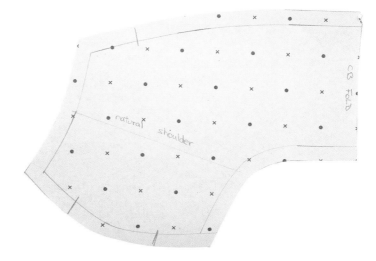

10 This design has a front and back yoke, with no shoulder seam. To create this, first trace the armhole side of the yoke. Then, excluding the dart, move the tracing paper to the neck side of the dart and trace the rest of the yoke.

11 Move the front yoke piece to join the back yoke piece so that the shoulder seams touch, and continue tracing. When the whole pattern piece is complete, add the seam allowance and cut it out. Cut one pattern piece at a time, and check all the pattern pieces that go together to ensure that they fit. This is good practice—testing patterns at this stage can save you a great deal of time and fabric later.

Pattern notches and their uses

Notches are extremely important. They act as the "road signs" for making up your garment.

Notches are used to identify parts of the pattern that fit together, to help you assemble your garment easily and accurately. When transferring the information from the pattern, make small clips to the edge of the fabric (no more than ⅛in/2–3mm). Too many notches can weaken a fabric or, if used to liberally, can become confusing.
Notches can indicate the following:
- An ease allowance in a garment
- Where to stop and start gathers
- Center lines or fold lines
- Hem depths and cuffs
- Where a zipper stops
- The natural waist line
- The natural shoulder point
- A change in seam allowance width (industry)
- How to match curved seams.

Although both commercial patterns and industry patterns have notches, they may look different on the patterns. Commercial pattern notches are indicated by triangles; industry notches are indicated by a "T" shape and then cut out as a nick with a pattern notcher. When drafting your own patterns, you will need to put notches on at the pattern plan stage. With a ruler, draw short lines that intersect both pattern pieces at right angles to the line being notched. The notches need to be traced through to all following pattern stages. Check that they match up.

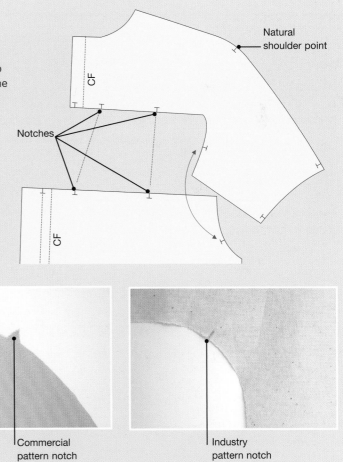

Natural shoulder point

CF

Notches

CF

Commercial pattern notch

Industry pattern notch

Simple dart manipulation

Darts are needed to turn two-dimensional shapes into three-dimensional shapes and to fit clothes closely to the body.

Once you understand the art of basic dart manipulation, you can look at any design and manipulate the block to achieve shape, a good silhouette, or design interest. Manipulating the bust dart is the first lesson in learning to cut patterns.

Different dart locations
Darts can be located in a number of different places on a bodice to alter its style.

Basic dart manipulation

The diagram above shows different dart locations. You can practice these dart manipulations as an exercise using either full-size or half-scale blocks. By moving these darts around the bust point, you will begin to understand the method. Using the basic bodice block (see pages 112–125), follow the step-by-step exercise below. The basic bodice has two darts. Start by consolidating the two darts into one side seam dart.

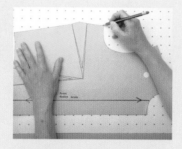

1 Trace off the front bodice; here the bodice block is made from cardstock, making tracing easier and more accurate.

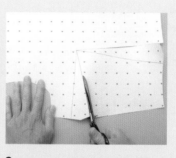

2 Cut up the front waist dart and the side seam dart.

3 Close the waist dart, and the side seam dart opens. (Remember not to cut right through; keep a small amount of paper attached to act as a hinge.)

To continue this exercise, trace off the front bodice block onto paper. Draw in the lines to the bust point as shown on the diagram. To manipulate the darts, simply slash to the apex each time, and then close and open the darts in different locations.

Asymmetric darts

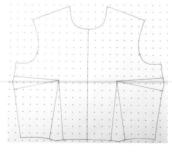

1 To create asymmetric darts, trace off the bodice block fronts, joining the right and left sides at the CF. The full bodice is traced off because the right and left sides are to be different.

2 Cut up both waist and side darts to the apexes. Close the bust dart until its edges meet. The waist darts will open.

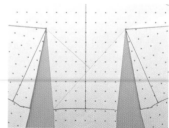

3 Draw in the new dart lines.

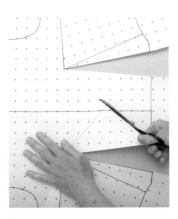

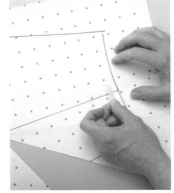

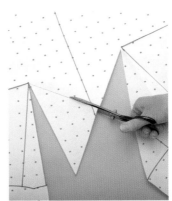

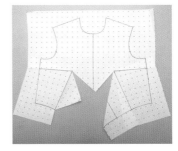

4 First cut along the long line that passes from left to right.

5 Close the right-hand waist dart, and the long dart opens.

6 Cut up the shorter dart and close the left-hand waist dart. The short dart opens.

7 The pattern development is complete. Trace in new darts and back away from the apex by 1½in (4cm). This is now your pattern plan. Trace this off onto a clean sheet of pattern tracing paper. Now you can add your seam allowance, notches, and grain lines.

Changing darts into gathers

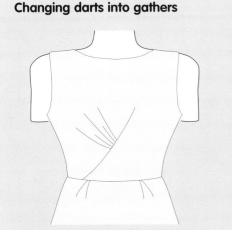

This style has gathering located under the bust instead of the dart. First, repeat the first six steps from "Asymmetric darts," above.

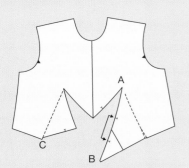

Measure the right-hand dart from A to B. Including the dart, the measurement will be longer from A to C; gather the excess fullness between the notches to match the shorter side as shown.

Changing one dart into three small darts

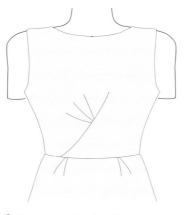

1 First, repeat the first five steps from "Asymmetric darts," above.

2 Draw in two darts on either side of the short central dart and cut them both up to the apex at an angle similar to the original dart. (Left side.) Leave the pattern paper slightly attached by a thin hinge of paper.

3 Cut up the three new darts. Close the left-hand waist dart to open the three darts by equal amounts. Mark the ends of the darts 1½in (4cm) back from the apex. Once completed, fold the paper to ensure that the darts are aligned with each other.

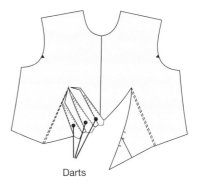

Darts

How to turn bodice darts into seams

The following exercises will teach you how to change darts into seams. The darts are moved away from the traditional bodice positions, while still retaining the bust suppression.

Princess seams

This is a standard pattern shape in which the bust darts are changed into seams. Both front and back seams start mid-shoulder and continue down to the waist line.

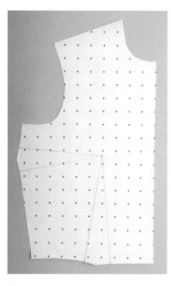

1 Trace the front bodice block.

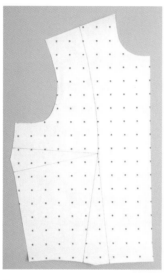

2 Using a skirt curve, mark out the design line on the front bodice. Start at the waist dart, pass through the bust apex, and go up to the center shoulder. This is the princess line.

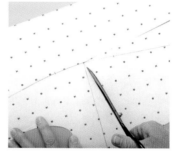

3 Cut up the waist dart and the side seam dart. Notch the pattern 2in (5cm) above and below the apex along the princess line.

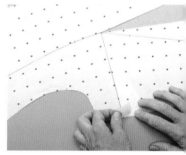

4 Close the side seam dart and the waist dart will open.

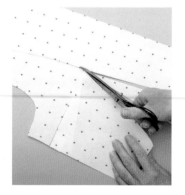

5 Cut up the other side of the waist dart.

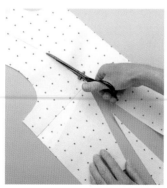

6 Cut through the apex and continue up into the shoulder.

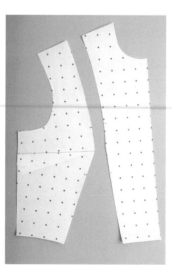

7 The front bodice is now ready to be traced off and seam allowance added. If the back bodice also has a princess line, it is made in the same way, but this time there is no bust dart to close. Just connect the waist dart to the shoulder dart, making sure both front and back seam lines match at the shoulder. Mark in notches (see page 83). Use double notches to indicate the back bodice.

Bodice without side seams

This top has no side seams. The seams have been moved away from the natural side seam at the front and back to create a side panel. Though similar to the pattern on page 86, these seam lines do not go to the apex. The fullness, therefore, is not directly over the fullest part of the bust where it is needed. For this pattern, a very small dart is left in to complete the bust suppression. If the dart was not required, the excess fabric could be eased in, still achieving the fit.

First, take your front and back bodice blocks and trace them off onto pattern tracing paper. Transfer all the darts and written information—CF, CB, etc. Remember to leave the seam allowances off at this stage so that you can manipulate your pattern more accurately.

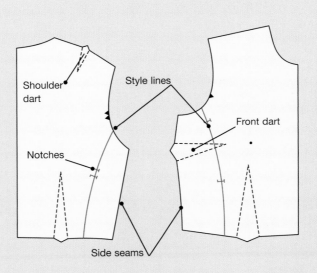

Shoulder dart

Style lines

Front dart

Notches

Side seams

1 Draw in the style lines within 2in (5cm) of the original side seams, front and back. Create notches: two single notches on the front, 2in (5cm) on either side of the dart, and one double notch on the back.

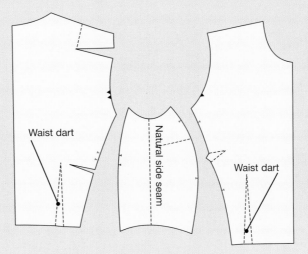

2 Cut along the style lines, close the front dart, and join the front and back pieces at the side seam to create a single side panel. Close the shoulder dart, opening it into the armhole.

Waist dart

Natural side seam

Waist dart

3 Close the front and back waist darts by half their width, putting the excess into the panel seams. This makes the main back body slightly longer, for ease. The front central panel excess can be made into the dart.

Styling sleeves and cuffs

Add details and shaping to sleeves and cuffs to create different styles.

Take your sleeve block and trace it off onto pattern tracing paper, transferring all the dart information, elbow line, notches, and so on. Remember, the front of the sleeve is indicated by one notch, the back by two, and these then correspond to the correct position on the bodice. Leave seam allowances off at this stage so that you can manipulate your pattern more accurately.

Removing the sleeve elbow dart

The sleeve block in this book has an elbow dart. The dart allows for room to move and bend the arm while retaining a close fitted shape to the sleeve. The dart can be removed as shown, but the sleeve will be less fitted.

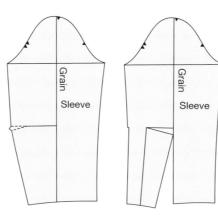

1 Trace out the darted block sleeve pattern. Draw a line from the end of the elbow dart at right angles to the straight grain line.

2 Cut up the straight grain line from the sleeve hem and across to the end of the elbow dart.

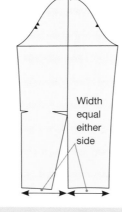

3 Cut along the dart from the underarm seam, but keep a hinge at the end of the dart. Pivot the dart closed, allowing the sleeve hem to open until the sleeve width measures equally on either side of the grain line. The sleeve is now wider at the wrist.

Adding fullness as gathers to the sleeve head

When adding fullness to a sleeve head it is good practice to shorten the bodice shoulder length by ⅜in (1cm) while adding ⅜in (1cm) to the sleeve head. This alteration helps to support the sleeve and keep it from dropping. The amount of this alteration can be changed according to the design and should be done first, along with deciding where the gathering is to be (see "Adding fullness," page 94).

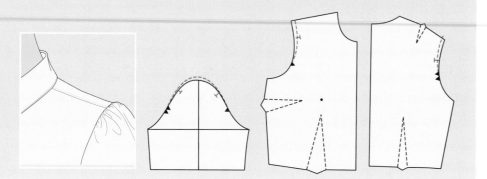

Half-circle sleeve

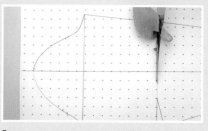

The basic principles shown here can be used with any length of sleeve.

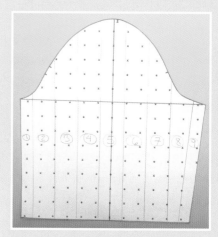

1 Trace around the sleeve block and shorten to the desired length.

2 Divide the sleeve into nine equal sections. Number each section in order.

Special note

If the design requires more fullness at either the front or the back, the pattern can be adjusted accordingly. Spread the sections out to the required width where the adjustment is needed (see page 94).

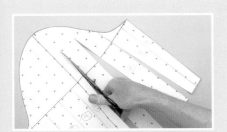

3 Cut up to each line but not through, keeping the sleeve cap edge intact.

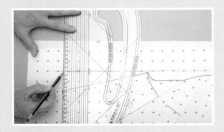

4 Next, on a separate piece of paper, draw out a large "T" shape. Place the cut sleeve onto it, aligning the underarm points to the "T." Secure the top pattern to the paper, trying to keep the distances between each section even.

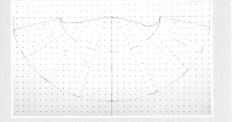

5 To mark the hemline, start by squaring off from the "T" at a right angle and continue along the sleeve length, smoothing out the hem.

6 This is your pattern plan. Trace off, adding seam allowance and a grain line.

Puffed sleeve head

This design has fullness only at the sleeve head. To help support the puff sleeve, shorten the shoulder line by ⅜in (1cm) (see "Adding fullness as gathers to the sleeve head," opposite).

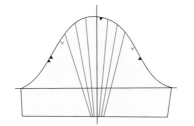

1 On a separate piece of paper, draw out a "T" shape. Decide on the position of the gathers. Divide this area up into six sections. The amount added between the pieces is dependent on the fullness required and the fabric used (see page 94).

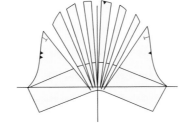

2 Align the biceps line of the sleeve on the "T" line with the vertical line in the center. Slash and spread the six sleeve sections from the sleeve head to the hem; do not cut through, but leave paper hinges.

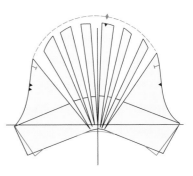

3 Add 1in (2.5cm) or more to the height of the sleeve head and draw a smooth line back to the original sleeve pattern. Transfer the shoulder notch to the new sleeve head. The sleeve hem could be tightened further through the underarm seam as indicated.

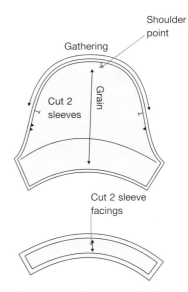

4 Add the seam allowance to the finished pattern and notch where the gathering is required on the sleeve head. To finish the curved hem of this sleeve, a facing will be required. (See "Facings and waistbands," page 105.)

Short puff sleeve with narrow cuff and keyhole opening

For this design, a "keyhole" opening is used. A "keyhole" is a simple way of constructing a cuff sleeve opening. Cut a straight line 3in (8cm) long from the sleeve end, in line with the elbow to where the cuff is to be attached. A bias strip of fabric is then sewn to the opening (see page 129).

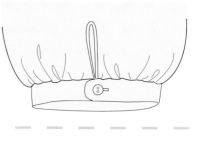

This sleeve has gathering both at the sleeve head and into the cuff. Here there is an equal number of gathers at each end; however, this is variable depending on the individual design. This short cuff (2in/5cm) needs an extra keyhole opening on the sleeve to allow the arm to fit through.

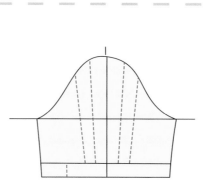

1 Decide on the sleeve length and draw in the cuff band. Divide the central part of the main sleeve into four equal parts. The red lines indicate where the gathering will be on the sleeve. It is important to make notches to identify the shoulder point and where the gathers stop and start on the bodice armhole. Number the four parts and cut them into separate sections.

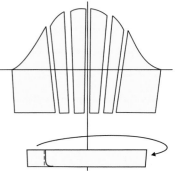

2 On a separate sheet of pattern paper, draw a vertical line and square across it to make a "T." Position your cut and numbered sleeve sections on the paper, spacing them equally and keeping the biceps line aligned to the horizontal "T" on the paper. Again, the amount added between the pieces is dependent on the fullness required and the fabric used. (See "Adding fullness," page 94.)

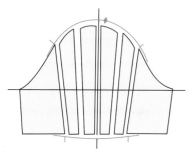

3 Smooth out the sleeve head and hem by re-drawing the lines. In these instances, you should always add. If the excess is not needed, it can be cut off later.

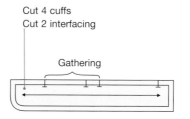

Cut 4 cuffs
Cut 2 interfacing

Gathering

4 Shape one end of the cuff and extend it by 1½in (4cm). This measurement is variable depending on the size of the button. (See "Buttons and buttonholes," page 101.)

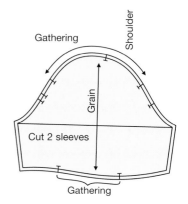

Gathering   Shoulder

Grain

Cut 2 sleeves

Gathering

5 Finished puff sleeve pattern with a shaped cuff.

Note

If this cuff had straight edges, it could simply be cut on the fold and sewn at the ends, and only one pattern piece would be needed. Because the end is shaped, however, two pattern pieces must be cut and interfacing applied on one side before the pieces are sewn together (see page 105).

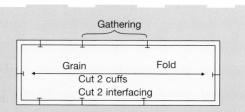

Gathering

Grain   Fold

Cut 2 cuffs
Cut 2 interfacing

Cuff cut on the fold with no shaping

Bell sleeve with gathers into a deep cuff

This sleeve has a 4in (10cm) deep cuff with buttons and buttonholes. The depth of the cuff means that there is plenty of room for the hand to pass through, with no need for an extra opening. The sleeve gathers into the cuff all the way around and is fuller at the back to allow room for the elbow. You will need to remove the elbow dart on the sleeve block to make this pattern (see page 88).

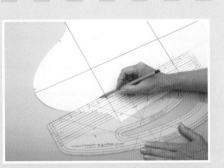

1 Trace off the sleeve block and remove the elbow dart (see page 88). Divide the sleeve into equal quarters lengthwise.

2 Measure up the grain line marking a cuff depth of 4in (10cm). Cut off the cuff.

3 Cut up the sleeve divisions to the sleeve cap edges, leaving hinges.

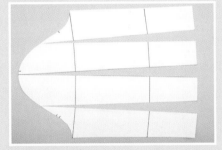

4 Open out the pieces by equal amounts to achieve the desired amount of sleeve fullness. (Use the ratio information on page 94 as a guide.)

5 Add paper underneath and redraw, smoothing out the sleeve hem edge. Add ½in (1.3cm) to the sleeve length at the elbow position and smooth back into the sleeve hem.

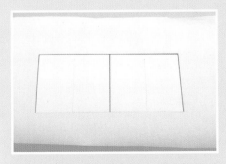

6 To construct the cuff, use the removed portion of the sleeve.

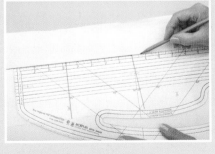

7 Extend the edge of the cuff by approximately ¾in (2cm), depending on the size of the buttons you are using.

8 The finished cuff with extension, indicating where the buttons and buttonholes are to be positioned.

Raglan sleeve

A raglan sleeve is a useful style that you may want to return to, so, once you have drafted your sleeve, it is a good idea to copy and save it as a working block. To make a standard raglan working block use the measurements given here. These can be altered for individual designs later.

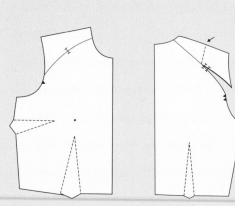

1 On the bodice, measure from the front neck shoulder point toward the CF 2in (5cm) and 3½in (9cm) toward the CB for the back neck. Connect this point with a line to the armhole to just above the notches. Slash and close the back shoulder dart, opening up the raglan shape.

⅜in (1cm)

2 Move the shoulder line forward by taking ⅜in (1cm) off the front and adding it to the back.

4in (10cm)   ⅜in (1cm)

⅜in (1cm)

Grain

3 On the sleeve, move the grain line toward the front by ⅜in (1cm) (indicated by a single notch). Next make a mark 4in (10cm) down from the sleeve head. Mark a point ⅜in (1cm) up from the sleeve head and square across.

4 Cut off the front and back shoulder sections from the bodice and place them so that the shoulder points are touching the ⅜in (1cm) line on the sleeve head. Allow the outside edge to blend into the sleeve just above the notches, in a similar position to where they were drawn on the bodice.

5 Blend the shoulder lines into the new sleeve grain line and then from the shoulder point to the 4in (10cm) point. Smooth out the new armhole lines. Measure these lines and compare them to the bodice armhole. The back sleeve is often slightly longer than the back bodice armhole—this is ease, and must be no more than ⅜in (1cm).

Grain   Grain

Note
Trace off the pattern at this stage for a one-piece raglan sleeve with a shoulder dart.

6 Separate the front and back sleeves along the new grain line, marking in the biceps line and all the notches. Make sure the shoulder edges are smooth.

Styling skirts

Try making these different skirt shapes and styles.

For each of these designs, you will need to take your front and back skirt blocks and trace them onto pattern tracing paper, transferring all the dart information. Remember to leave seam allowances off at this stage so that you can manipulate your pattern more accurately.

Lengthening a skirt
When lengthening an A-line skirt, the longer the skirt, the fuller the hem will become. If you want to achieve a slinkier silhouette, you could place the skirt on the bias (see page 41).

A-line skirt

The A-line skirt is a classic but simple style. It is fitted around the waist and hips through the use of darts, and flare is added evenly at the hem to produce a well-balanced bell-like shape.

1 Draw a line from the dart's end to the hem. Repeat for the back of the skirt.

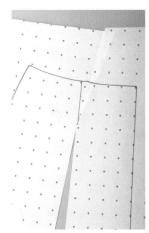

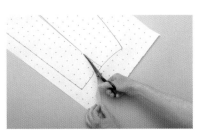

2 Slash up the lines from the hem to the dart ends, and from the waist down. Do not cut through the end of the dart; keep a small amount of paper attached as a hinge.

4 Only half the amount of flare is added to the side seam front and back. These halves add up to make the whole amount at the side seam.

3 Decrease the darts while opening the hem for the desired amount of flare. The darts will be made smaller. To retain a well-balanced skirt add the same amount of flare front and back.

5 The complete skirt pattern. Remember to add seam allowance.

Flared skirt

The same principles and method applied to the A-line skirt are applied to the flared skirt, but with more flare added at the hem. The amount of flare added is a personal choice.

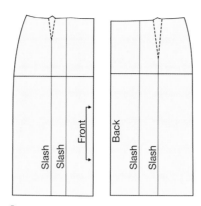

1 Trace off the skirt blocks (see pages 112–125). Draw a line parallel to the CF and CB from the waist to the hem. Draw a parallel line connecting the dart ends with the hem. Ideally the skirt should be split into three equal portions; this may depend on where the dart is positioned.

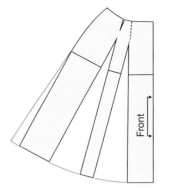
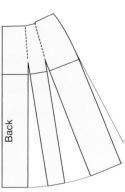

2 Slash up from the hem, closing the darts and opening the hem in equal proportions for the desired amount of flare, with half on the side seam front and back as before. Repeat for the back skirt. It is important to add the same amount front and back. By doing this you will retain the overall balance.

Adding fullness

Pattern cutting uses prescribed methods for adding fullness—flare, darts, gathers, or tucks—in which you can control where the fullness is created. This is known as slashing and spreading. This method is used for all garments, but is illustrated here using a skirt. The amount of fabric added is dependent on the type of fabric used and the silhouette required. The following ratios are a guideline only: Heavy denim or wool might be stiff and bulky, so using a ratio of 1½in (3.5cm) of fabric to 1in (2.5cm) of waistband or less might work best. Soft silks or fine jerseys might use a ratio of 4in (10cm) of fabric to every 1in (2.5cm) of waistband or more to create extra volume.

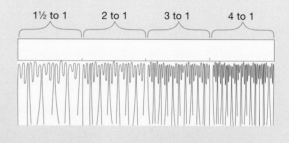

1½ to 1   2 to 1   3 to 1   4 to 1

Exercise 1: Even distribution of fullness

For fullness at waist and hem, draw and number equal sections on your pattern and cut apart. Draw a straight line on another piece of paper and align the pattern pieces to this, with equal spaces in between. If this pattern piece is shaped, numbering the pieces and drawing a line through them ensures that the amount added is in proportion.

Exercise 2: Increasing fullness on one edge of a pattern

Slash and spread the pattern on the edge requiring the fullness, leaving the other edge as it was. By increasing fullness in this way, volume is added at the hem but not at the waist.

Exercise 3: Adding differing amounts of fullness

Quite simply, add more fullness where it is required.

Flared skirt with yoke

First work out the depth of the yoke and the hem circumference. This flared skirt has a shaped yoke. The skirt fits smoothly into the yoke except at the CF where it has a gathered section. There is a concealed zipper with a button and buttonhole at the CB yoke.

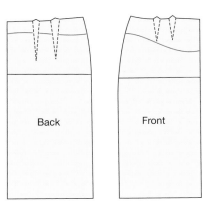

1 Trace off the skirt blocks and draw on your design lines. Make the yoke deeper in the front than the back and make sure the side seams match.

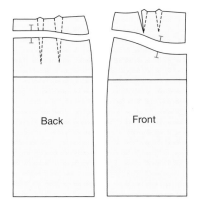

2 Notch the front, the back, and where the gathering is located, and cut the yoke away from the skirt.

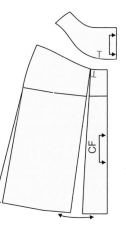

3 Slash and close the darts on the front yoke. Slash and spread the skirt. The first slash will be 2in (5cm) at the hem plus 2in (5cm) at the top as fullness for the gathering. This measurement can vary, depending on the design.

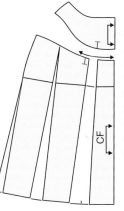

4 Continue slashing and spreading. Remember to add only half the amount (1in/2.5cm) at the side seam hem front and back to a total of 2in (5cm) at side seam.

Tip

• If the darts don't completely close when spreading the pattern, and the amount left is no more than 3/8in (1cm), take 3/16in (0.5cm) off the side seam and leave 3/16in (0.5cm) as ease.

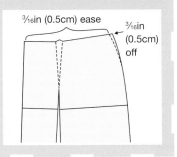

3/16in (0.5cm) ease

3/16in (0.5cm) off

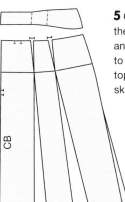

5 Close the darts on the back yoke. Slash and spread from hem to dart ends and to the top edge. Open the skirt hem to 2in (5cm).

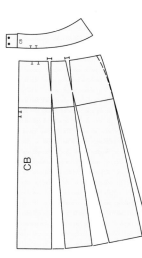

6 If the darts do not close completely, shave 3/8in (1cm) off the skirt waist edge and blend in the line. Extend the CB yoke to accommodate buttons and buttonholes.

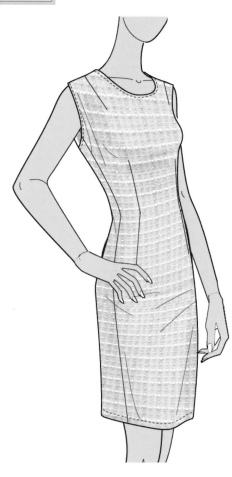

Styling dresses

You can join skirt and bodice blocks to make a dress block.

Many different garments can be created by joining a bodice block and a skirt block, from dresses to hip-length blouses and shirts.

The dress block is a combination of the bodice and skirt block and a versatile foundation to making many other patterns. Because there is no waist seam, fit is achieved through torso darts and side seams.

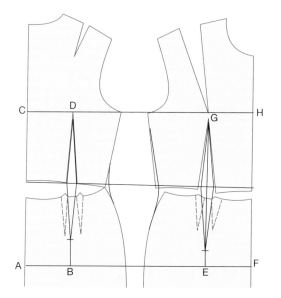

The torso block

The torso block is a bodice block that extends down to the hip line. This is a useful block in its own right for drafting garments with a defined waist line, such as the blouse on page 81. Many patterns can be made from this one simple block, including jackets, gowns, and coats.

The torso block is simply a shortened version of the dress block and can be used to make a dress block by extending the CF and CB lines and the side seams 27½in (70cm) downward from the CB waist to the finished hem.

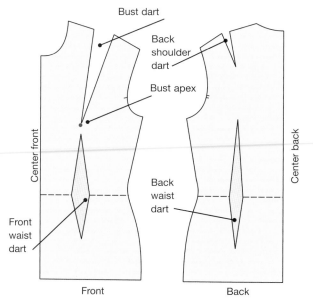

The torso block

Bust dart

Back shoulder dart

Bust apex

Center front

Front waist dart

Back waist dart

Center back

Front

Back

Drafting the dress block

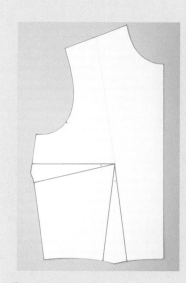

1 Trace off the bodice block front and draw in a new dart position from the shoulder to the bust point.

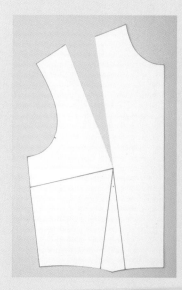

2 Cut down the shoulder line to the bust point, and from the side seam dart to the bust point. Leave a hinge.

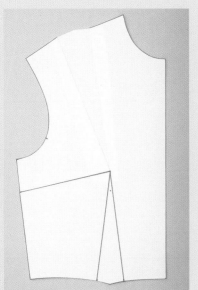

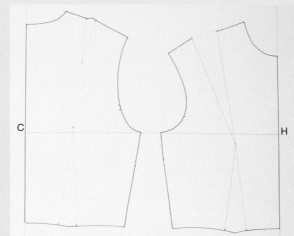

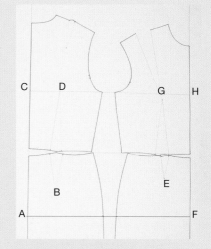

3 Close the side seam bust dart and open the shoulder dart. Trace off and use this block for making a dress block.

4 Using this new front and back bodice, square a line across at chest level, using the side seam underarm point (line CH on diagram). When drafting this pattern, draw a long line on the left-hand side of the pattern paper and line the CB of the bodice onto it. Leave a 4in (10cm) gap before placing the front bodice on the pattern paper. Once this is done, extend the CF line downward, using a long ruler.

5 Place the CB and CF of the back and front skirt blocks on your long lines so that the side waist points are touching the bodice waist line. The skirt waist shaping is such that the CF and CB points won't touch. Square across from the CB bodice waist line to the CF, making a new waist line. Measure 8in (20cm) down from this to create a new hip line (line AF).

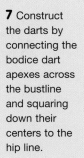

6 Blend and smooth out the side seam of the back bodice. Starting at the armhole, take 3/8in (1cm) off the front bodice waist line, blending the side seams into the skirt.

7 Construct the darts by connecting the bodice dart apexes across the bustline and squaring down their centers to the hip line.

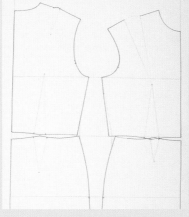

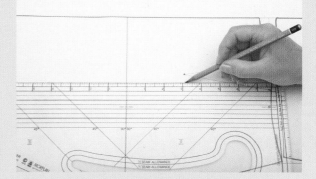

8 Measure 3in (8cm) back up the line from the hip line (at B on diagram) to mark the end of the back dart. Measure 4in (10cm) up from the hip line (at E on diagram) to mark the end of the front dart.

This sequence continues on the next page ➤

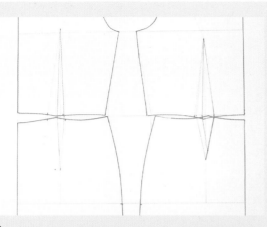

9 Construct the darts at the waist line, 1½in (4cm) wide for the front dart, ¾in (2cm) on either side of the central line, 1in (2.5cm) for the back dart, and ½in (1.25cm) on either side of the central line.

10 Trace around the outside edge of the pattern, marking in the new bust, waist, and hip lines, the new single waist dart, and the shoulder darts. This is your completed dress block. No seam allowance should be added. Now trace it onto cardstock.

Princess line dress

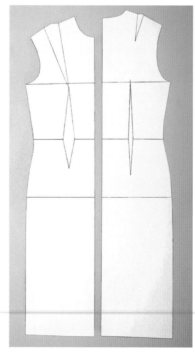

1 Trace off and cut out the dress block.

The princess line dress is made by turning the darts of the dress block into long seams. Using these seams it is easy to add flare at the hem. Flare can be added from the waist line, hip line, or knee. Each point will produce a very different style.

2 Mark out the design lines. Start at the waist dart and pass through the bust apex up to the center shoulder.

3 From the base of the waist dart draw a line parallel to the CF down to the hemline. Repeat for the back. This is the princess line.

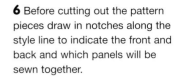

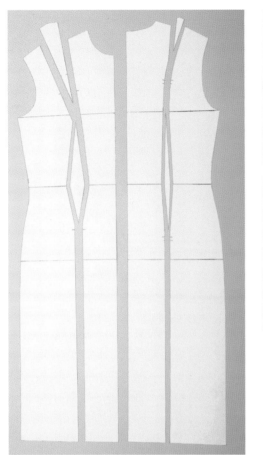

6 Before cutting out the pattern pieces draw in notches along the style line to indicate the front and back and which panels will be sewn together.

7 When all pattern pieces are cut out, match up the notches and square off the hemline.

4 Cut the front and back panels into separate pieces as shown. Stick the four main panels onto a paper base, aligning the hip and waist lines and leaving about 4in (10cm) between each panel.

5 To add flare, decide how much you would like to add, and from which point—waist, hip, or knee—and add the same amount to each seam.

8 The completed pattern. Remember to add seam allowances, grain lines (90 degrees to the waist line), and all other pattern information.

Collar styles

Different collar shapes can be added to your bodices to create different styles.

When adding a collar to a garment, you need to consider both how it will be attached to the bodice and how it will be finished inside the neck of the garment.

Drafting a collar pattern

When drafting a collar pattern, make any neckline alterations to the bodice pattern beforehand. To measure the bodice neckline accurately, first match up the garment shoulder lines. Measure from the CB neck to the CF neck holding the tape measure on its edge (see right). This allows the tape to bend naturally around the curves, ensuring a more accurate measurement and improving the collar's fit. You may need to adjust the collar pattern when toiling if the fabric is thick or if it stretches.

Consider how your collar will be finished on the inside of the garment. Look at your design and make a working drawing. A collar ending at the CF point may need a facing to finish the inside neck (see page 105). If the collar extends to the garment edge, all seam allowances will push up inside the collar itself to finish the edges.

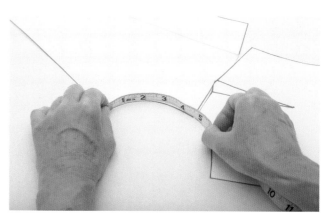

Measure the neckline
Measure the collar from CB neck to CF neck with the tape measure on its side.

Top collars and under collars

When constructing collar patterns it is important to remember that all collars have a top and an under collar. This finishes the collar edge and eliminates bulk. The top collar has farther to travel from the neck edge to the collar edge. The under collar has a shorter distance to travel.

The amount by which the under collar should be shorter is dependent on the thickness of the fabric. Start with $\frac{1}{8}$in (3mm) shorter and try the collar out. (For sewing instructions see page 137.) To make the under collar, shorten the depth by $\frac{1}{8}$in (3mm) at the CB neck, continue with the $\frac{1}{8}$in (3mm) past the shoulder notch, and gently blend into the CF neck edge.

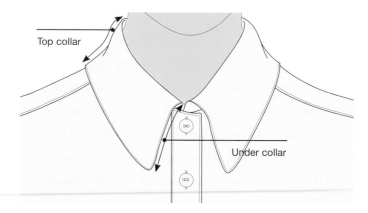

Collar terminology

Collar edge
This is the outside edge of a collar. Its shape helps determine how the collar sits on the body. The straighter the outside edge, the closer the collar will sit to the neck.

Collar stand
The collar stand is the part that rests closest to the neck.

Roll line
The roll line is the fold between the collar stand and the outer face of the collar (the part that you see).

Neck edge
This is the part of the collar that is attached to the garment neck. Its shaping is important and affects how the finished collar looks.

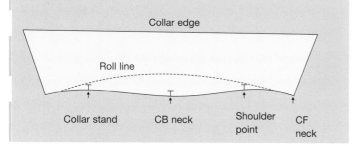

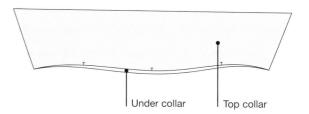

Buttons and buttonholes

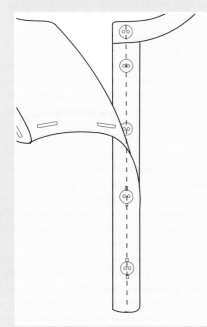

What is the button wrap?

A button wrap is an extension of both garment fronts to allow for button and buttonhole fastenings. The width of the wrap is dependent on the size of the button and the direction of the buttonholes. Vertical buttonholes may require less width than horizontal buttonholes.

How big should the buttonhole be?

The buttonhole size is determined by not only the button size but also its thickness, the fabric used, and whether the button has a shank. As a general rule, the size of the buttonhole is the diameter of the button plus 1/8in (3mm). Before making any buttonholes in a garment it is good practice to do a test on a sample of your chosen fabric. The test piece should have the same number of layers as your garment, for example, two of fabric and one of interfacing.

Positioning the buttons: things to consider

- Try to arrange the button placement so that one button is level with the bust point. This avoids gaping across the chest.

- If your garment has a Rever collar (a collar with lapels turned back to show the reverse side), place a button at the break point so that it closes in the correct place.

- When placing buttons on a shirt collar or collar stand, the buttonhole is usually positioned horizontally. The buttonholes on the placket should be vertical.

- The buttons in horizontally placed buttonholes do not sit in the middle. When a buttoned garment is worn, the button will always pull to the end of its buttonhole. The center of the button needs to sit on the CF line, so the buttonhole needs to be stitched backward, away from the garment edge.

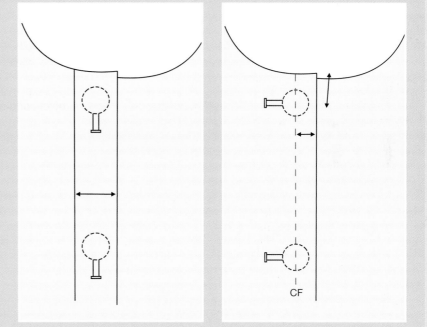

Opening with a placket

When a front opening has a placket or stitch line, the buttonhole direction must be vertical. This way the buttonhole will not interrupt the placket width or the topstitching

Opening without a placket

When an opening does not have stitching or a placket, the buttonhole direction is horizontal. The buttonhole at the very edge of the garment should be positioned carefully, so that the button does not protrude over the edge of the fabric when done up.

Basic one-piece shirt collar

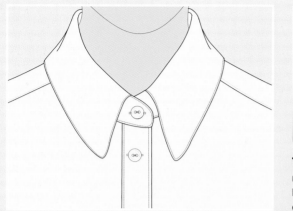

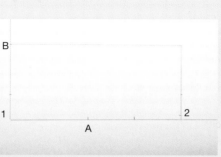

This basic shirt collar draft is for a one-piece collar, which can be adapted to a two-piece shirt collar.

1 Draft out a rectangle half of the full neck measurement from (1) to (2). Measure the back bodice neck length from the CB (1) to determine the shoulder point (A). Point B is the collar depth plus the collar stand depth, which may vary according to the design.

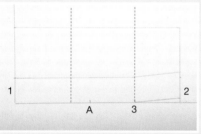

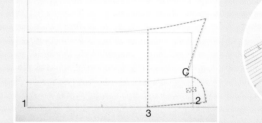

2 Start shaping the collar. First, to find point 3, divide the length of the collar equally into thirds (point 3 lies where the last third begins). Then, measure up ¼in (0.5cm) from the CF point (2), and connect back to (3). This creates the front shaping for the neck.

3 The lower section of the collar is the collar stand, which is half the collar width minus ⅜in (1cm). Square a line across from the CB. Extend the line from (3) to (2) and beyond the CF by half the button wrap measurement. Start to shape the lower front third of the collar as shown in red. At point (C) back away from the CF line by ⅛in (3mm) to create the stand shaping.

4 From point (C) extend up and out to achieve the collar shaping as shown.

5 Cut the pattern out of muslin without a seam allowance, placing the CB on the fold to test the collar's shape and fit on the stand. It is helpful to mark out CB and CF lines on the muslin so that the collar's fit can be accurately assessed when toiling (see page 68). Slash into and correct the muslin collar and transfer any adjustments to your pattern. Add seam allowance and notches.

Two-piece collar

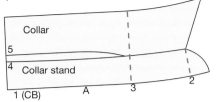

1 Trace off the one-piece collar, including the stand width line. Separate the stand from the collar at the CB by a ¼in (5mm) gap above the stand line (4) to (5). Connect the collar edge from (5) with a smooth curve back to the red line at (3).

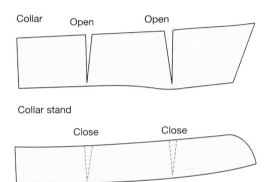

2 Separate the collar from the stand by tracing the pieces off separately. Shape the stand by dividing it into equal thirds, slash up the lines, and close ¼in (5mm) at the outside collar edge. Shape the collar by slashing and spreading the outside edge, this time adding in ¼in (0.5cm).

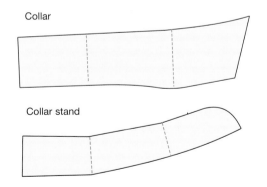

3 Cut both pattern pieces out of muslin, adding seam allowance only where the collar meets the stand so that they can be sewn together. Next mark out the CF and CB and try the pieces out on the dress stand. Look at the collar shape and make any adjustments. Once complete, transfer the pattern alterations to the new pattern, adding seam allowance, notches, and grain lines.

Mandarin collar

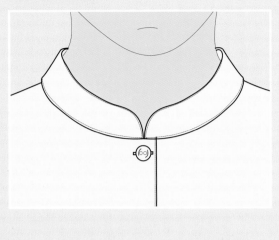

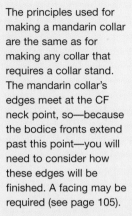

The principles used for making a mandarin collar are the same as for making any collar that requires a collar stand. The mandarin collar's edges meet at the CF neck point, so—because the bodice fronts extend past this point—you will need to consider how these edges will be finished. A facing may be required (see page 105).

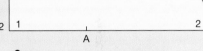

1 Draw out a rectangle half the full neck measurement from the CB to the CF (1 to 2). Measure the back neck length from the CB for the shoulder point at (A). Make the rectangle 1½in (4cm) in height. This measurement is variable, depending on the design.

2 Round off the CF top corner.

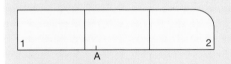

3 Divide the collar length into three equal pieces and cut from the collar edge to the neck edge, keeping a paper hinge.

4 Shape the collar by overlapping the cuts on the top edge by ¼in (0.5cm) each.

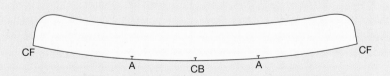

5 Trace the collar onto a piece of folded muslin to try out the shape on the dress stand—you don't need seam allowance for this. The process of cutting and overlapping or equally loosening the collar edge can be repeated if more or less shaping is required. Once you have the correct shape in the muslin, trace onto a new piece of paper, adding seam allowance and notching the CB, shoulder seams, and CF. The collar is now complete.

Peter Pan collar

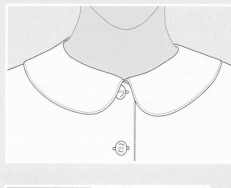

The Peter Pan collar demonstrates perfectly how a collar shape can relate to the neck and body. This collar can lay flat to the shoulder or, through slashing and overlapping the outside edges, start to roll around the neck. The basic principles are: the shorter the collar, the higher it will ride around the neck; the more curve a collar has, the flatter to the body it will sit.

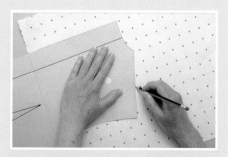

1 Trace around the back bodice block.

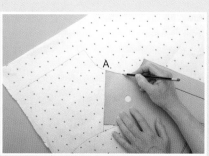

2 Place the front block pattern, matching it up to the back bodice at the shoulder neck point (A) and pivot the front shoulder to overlap the back by 2in (5cm). Draw in the neck edge.

3 Measure out 2in (5cm) from the neck edge to form the collar outside edge. As you approach the CF, draw in a round, smooth shape.

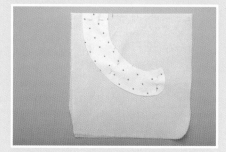

4 To test the collar shaping, place the CB on the fold and cut out the collar pattern without seam allowance on the outside edge only.

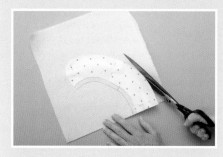

5 Add ⅜in (1cm) seam allowance to the neck edge only—this is for pinning the collar to the stand.

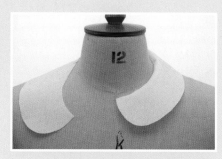

6 Pin the collar on the stand, starting at the CB neck and working around to the CF. Pin the collar from underneath so the collar rolls as if it were sewn to a garment.

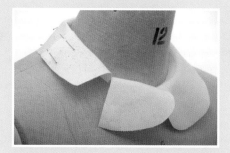

7 If the collar edge stands away from the neck, it is too long. To correct this, slash in and close the collar outside edge, by overlapping the muslin. Cut to the seam allowance and position the pins horizontally so they do not interfere with the collar roll.

8 The left side has been corrected and the collar now sits closer to the body. Take the collar off the stand and correct the pattern accordingly. Add seam allowance, grain lines, and other information.

Facings and waistbands

Facings can be used to finish off the edges of your garments.

Simple to construct, a facing is often merely a 1–2in (2–5cm) wide copy of the required edges of the original pattern piece. A facing can be used in many instances but is particularly useful on curves such as armholes, circular or curved hems, and necklines without collars—although necklines with collars sometimes also have facings. A facing can also be "grown on" to the pattern and folded into position. This is a method often found on shirts (see page 106).

Facings: things to consider

- Separate facing patterns need to be traced from the original pattern and marked with grain lines, notches, and seam allowance in order to construct the garment. Facings are always fused with interfacing; this helps to support buttons and buttonholes and stabilizes the garment, eliminating any stretching of the curved edges as they are sewn.

- When constructing the facings keep the outer edges smooth, without sharp angles. A facing should be invisible from the outside of the garment, so gentle curves that are sympathetic to the body are preferable.

- Seams can be eliminated from the facings to reduce bulk by simply combining neck and armhole facings.

- Consider how the garment will look when finished. For example, a back neck facing could be extended so the inside of the fabric is not seen when the garment is hung up. You may even wish to consider how a label might look on the facing.

Combined neck and armhole facing

Sometimes neck and armhole facings can be combined. This is a neat finish if both facings are required. It reduces fabric bulk and simplifies the making process.

1 Trace around the bodice front. Measure 2in (5cm) inward around the armhole and start to mark out your line.

2 Continue measuring 2in (5cm) from around the armhole to the shoulder and on to the neckline, blend the line together.

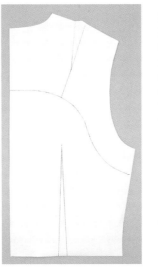

3 Repeat for the back. If your design has a shoulder dart, do not put the dart in the facing; remove it by slashing closed and transferring the dart fullness to the facing edge.

4 The finished neck and armhole facings for front and back.

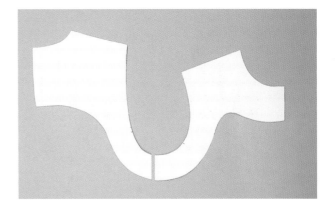

Grown-on facing

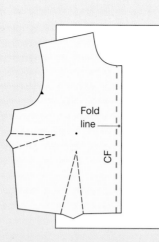

A grown-on facing is a quick and easy way to finish the front of a garment. It can be used when a collar needs to be joined to a neck, as it finishes the inside neck edge neatly. It is also a convenient way of creating a button wrap extension.

1 Trace around the bodice front, leaving plenty of spare paper beyond the CF line. Add half the width of the button wrap to the CF edge; this will become the fold line for the facing.

2 Flip the paper over on the new fold line to trace a mirror image of the front. This will become the facing. Draw red diagonal lines onto the pattern piece to indicate where the interfacing is to be placed.

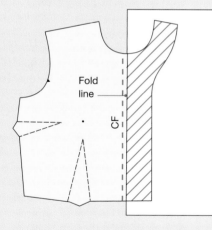

3 Add notches at the neck to indicate the CF for the collar and to indicate the fold line for the facing and interfacing placement.

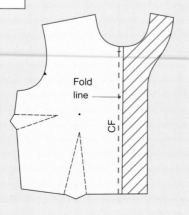

Skirt facing

A skirt facing is a simple method for finishing the waist line of a skirt. Alternatively you could use a waistband (see opposite).

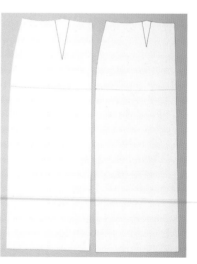

1 Start with the skirt pattern pieces to be faced, front and back.

2 Trace off the top sections of skirt, front and back. Slash down through the darts and continue to the paper edge. Close the darts, transferring the fullness to below the dart. Measure down 2in (5cm); this will be the finished width of the skirt facing.

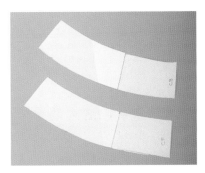

3 The finished skirt facings.

Straight waistband for pants and skirts

The quickest method for making a straight waistband is to cut it on the fold. A waistband can have CF, CB, or side opening. It is traditional for a side opening to be on the left. The waistband shown here is in one piece with a CF opening.

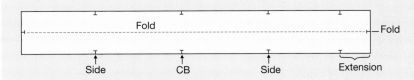

1 Make the waistband length the same as the garment waist measurement plus an extension for a button and buttonhole or hook and bar fastening.

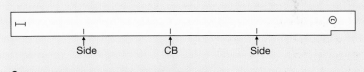

2 You will need to add seam allowance and ½in (1.3cm) ease—increase the amount of ease if the fabric is bulky or thick.

V-neck facing

Draw around the front and back bodice necklines. Next, draw in the front neck and the armhole facings with a finished width of 2in (5cm). The back neck facing should be made longer so that when the garment is on a hanger you can't see the wrong side of the fabric. This gives a more professional finish.

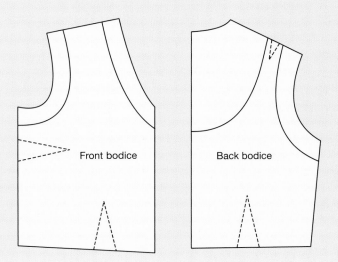

Front bodice Back bodice

Pocket styles

There are a variety of styles of pockets that you can add to garments for a different look or for practicality.

You may want to add pockets to your garment. These could be decorative or functional. On this spread are some examples of pockets that are easy to make.

Patch pockets

The patch pocket is the simplest kind of pocket to make. The pocket is made up beforehand with a hem at the top and all the edges turned under. It is then simply stitched onto the outside of the garment. See page 138 for instructions on how to sew on a patch pocket.

Patch pocket styles

Skirt side pockets

This classic pocket can be adapted to suit pants or skirts. The clever design of this pocket can be made to flatter the body by adapting the angle of the pocket opening, making the waist appear smaller.

1 Trace around the front skirt pattern block.

Side seam pockets

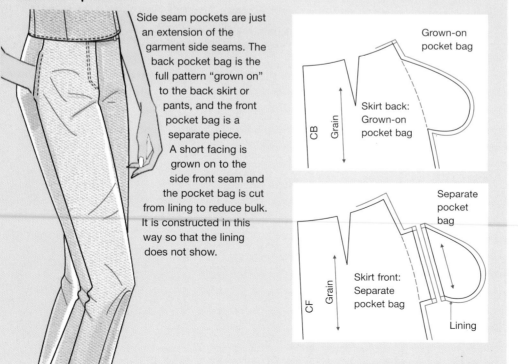

Side seam pockets are just an extension of the garment side seams. The back pocket bag is the full pattern "grown on" to the back skirt or pants, and the front pocket bag is a separate piece. A short facing is grown on to the side front seam and the pocket bag is cut from lining to reduce bulk. It is constructed in this way so that the lining does not show.

Grown-on pocket bag

CB Grain

Skirt back: Grown-on pocket bag

Separate pocket bag

CF Grain

Skirt front: Separate pocket bag

Lining

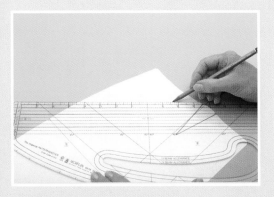

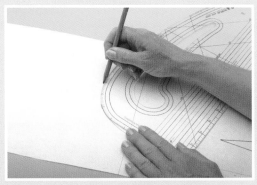

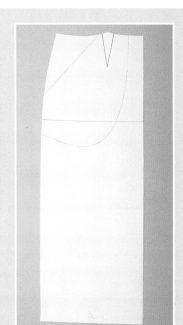

2 Measure down the side seam 7in (17cm) and along the waist line 4in (10cm) and connect with a line. This will be the pocket opening.

3 Draw out the pocket bag shape, using your hand as a guide for size and your pattern master or skirt curve for shape.

4 The finished pocket template.

5 Trace off the pocket template and slash down the skirt dart and close.

6 Transfer the dart fullness to the pocket outside edge. Add paper underneath.

7 Smooth out the pocket edge by redrawing it. Trace off both sides of the pocket bag. One side will be cut from lining; the other side can be cut from the same fabric as the skirt or be cut in lining fabric and have a facing piece.

8 The finished pattern pieces.

Finding a block in your size

The pattern blocks provided over the following pages are the standard sizes used by pattern companies; however, your figure shape may vary from those supplied, and further alterations may be needed. (See pages 72–79 for advanced pattern alterations.) If your sizing is different than the blocks in the book, using the hip and bust measurements, choose the block size closest to your own, or, if there is a choice pick the larger size block and reduce it. It is far easier to make a pattern smaller than larger. If you do not find the correct size in this book, most commercial pattern companies have special patterns catering to larger sizes.

The pattern blocks

In this chapter, you'll find basic pattern blocks for a skirt, bodice, and sleeves in US sizes 6–18 (UK 8–20). Scale the blocks up using the grid provided (see page 66) to make your own personalized pattern blocks, the building blocks from which you can design and make your own clothes.

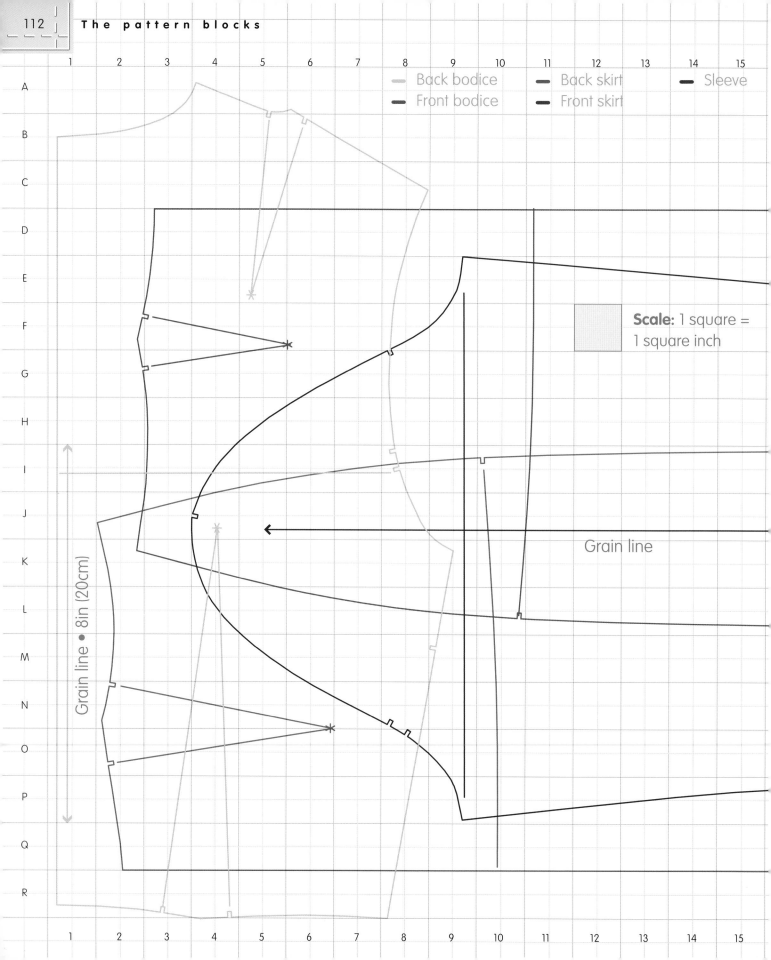

Back bodice
Front bodice
Back skirt
Front skirt
Sleeve

Scale: 1 square = 1 square inch

Grain line

Grain line • 8in (20cm)

US SIZE 6
pattern blocks

See page 66 for instructions on how to scale up the pattern blocks.

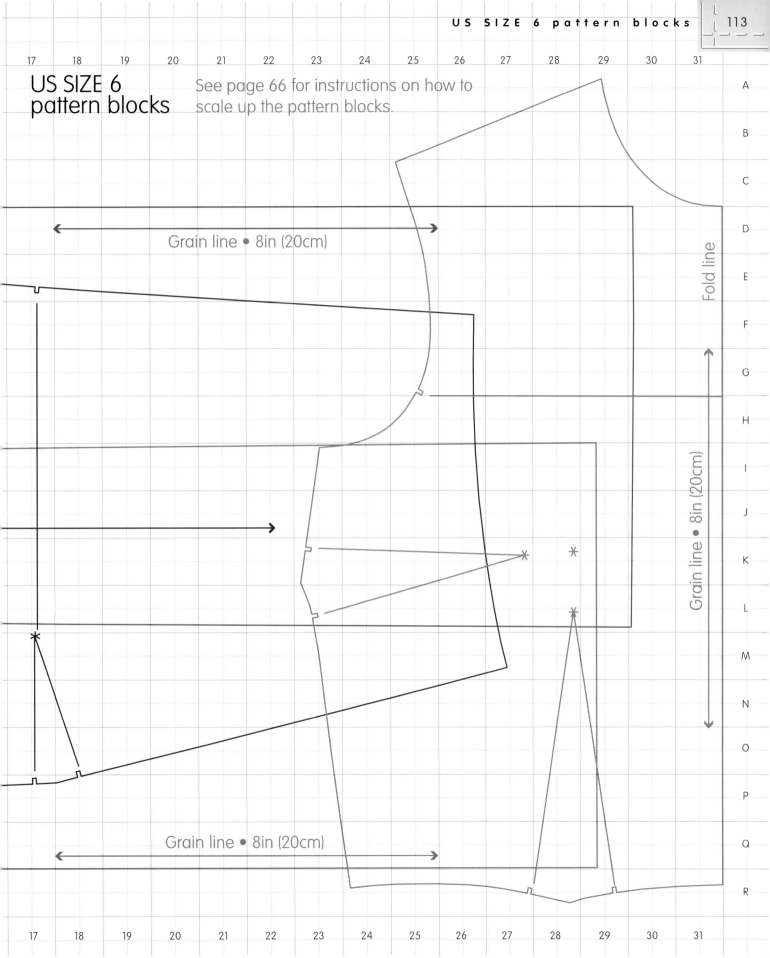

Grain line • 8in (20cm)

Fold line

Grain line • 8in (20cm)

Grain line • 8in (20cm)

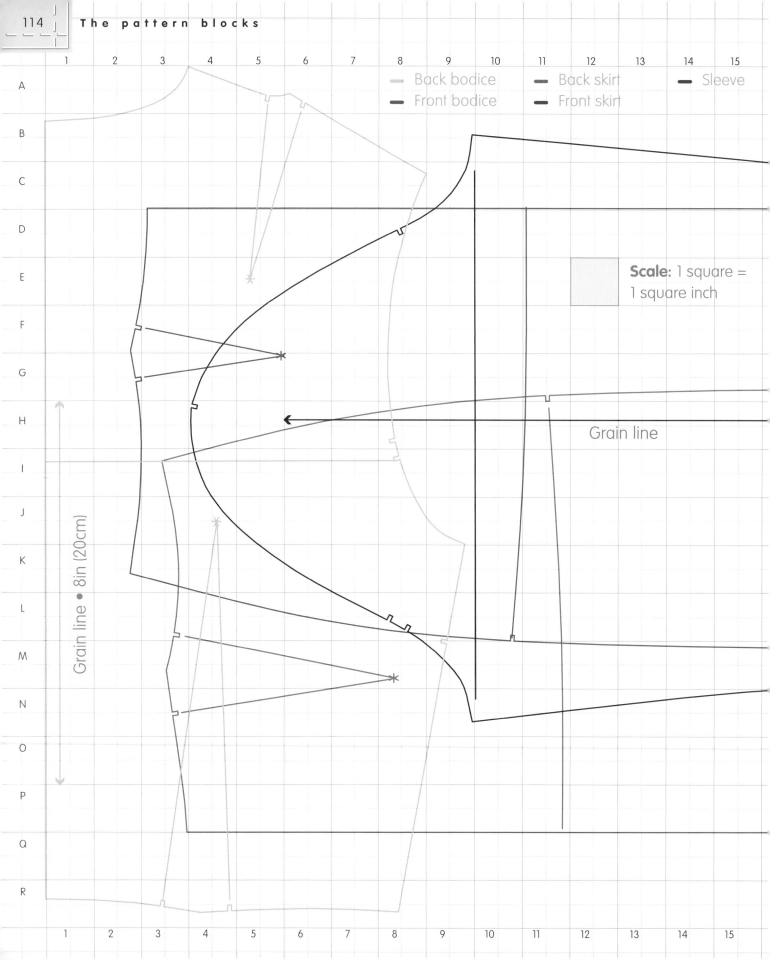

Back bodice   Back skirt   Sleeve
Front bodice   Front skirt

Scale: 1 square = 1 square inch

Grain line

Grain line • 8in (20cm)

17 18 19 20 21 22 23 24 25 26 27 28 29 30 31

US SIZE 8 pattern blocks

See page 66 for instructions on how to scale up the pattern blocks.

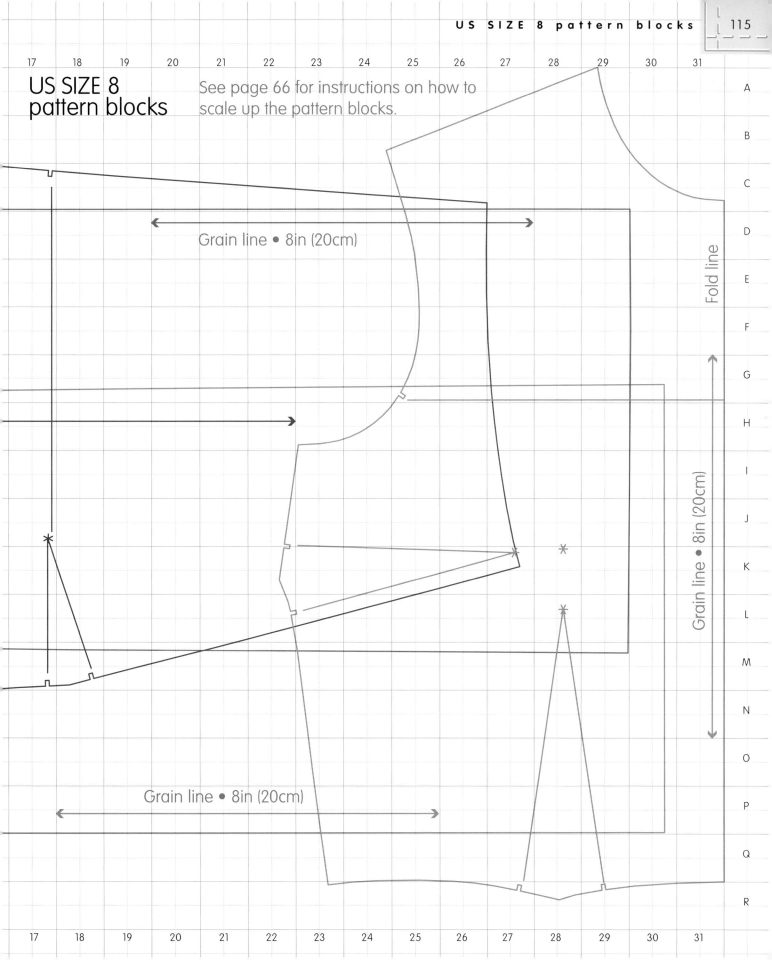

Grain line • 8in (20cm)

Fold line

Grain line • 8in (20cm)

Grain line • 8in (20cm)

A B C D E F G H I J K L M N O P Q R

17 18 19 20 21 22 23 24 25 26 27 28 29 30 31

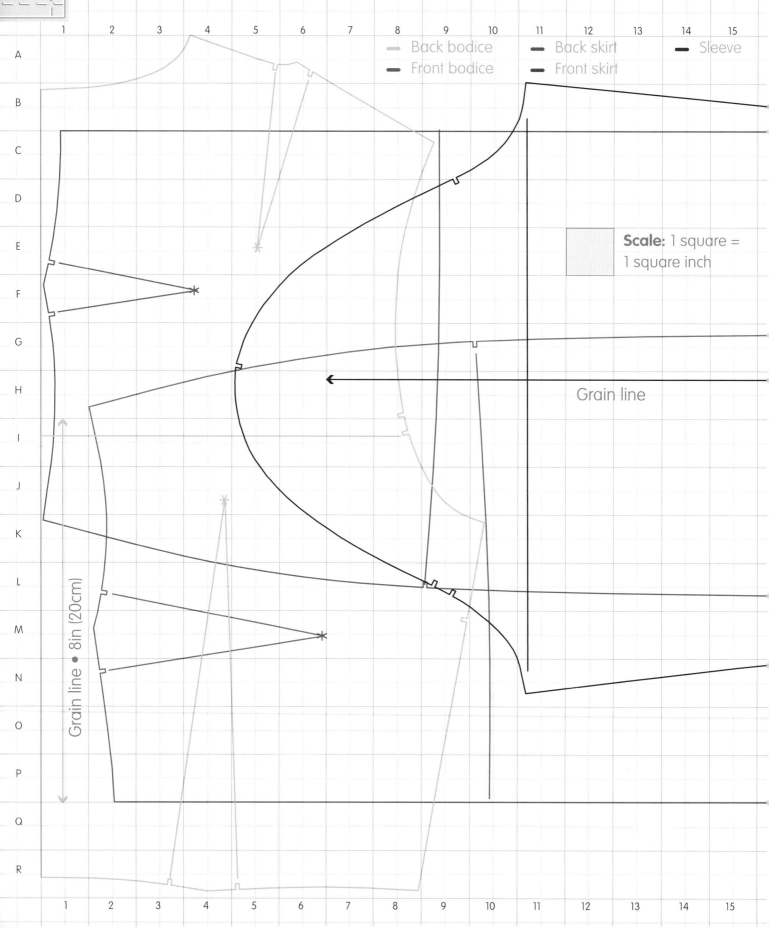

Scale: 1 square = 1 square inch

Back bodice
Front bodice
Back skirt
Front skirt
Sleeve

Grain line

Grain line • 8in (20cm)

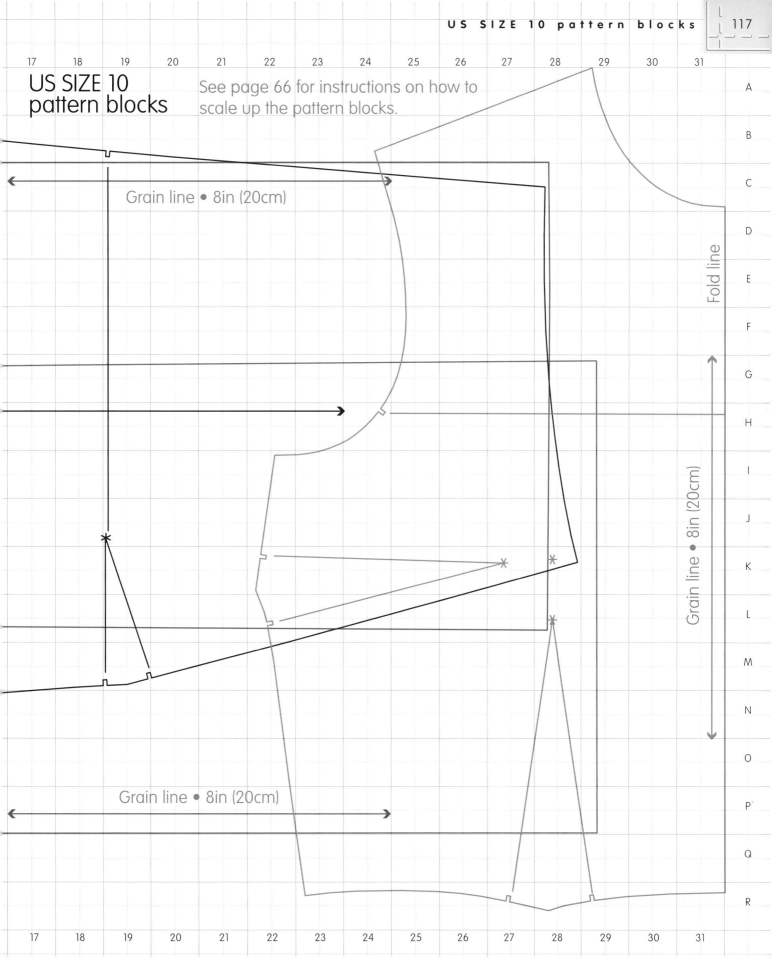

US SIZE 10 pattern blocks

See page 66 for instructions on how to scale up the pattern blocks.

Grain line • 8in (20cm)

Grain line • 8in (20cm)

Grain line • 8in (20cm)

Fold line

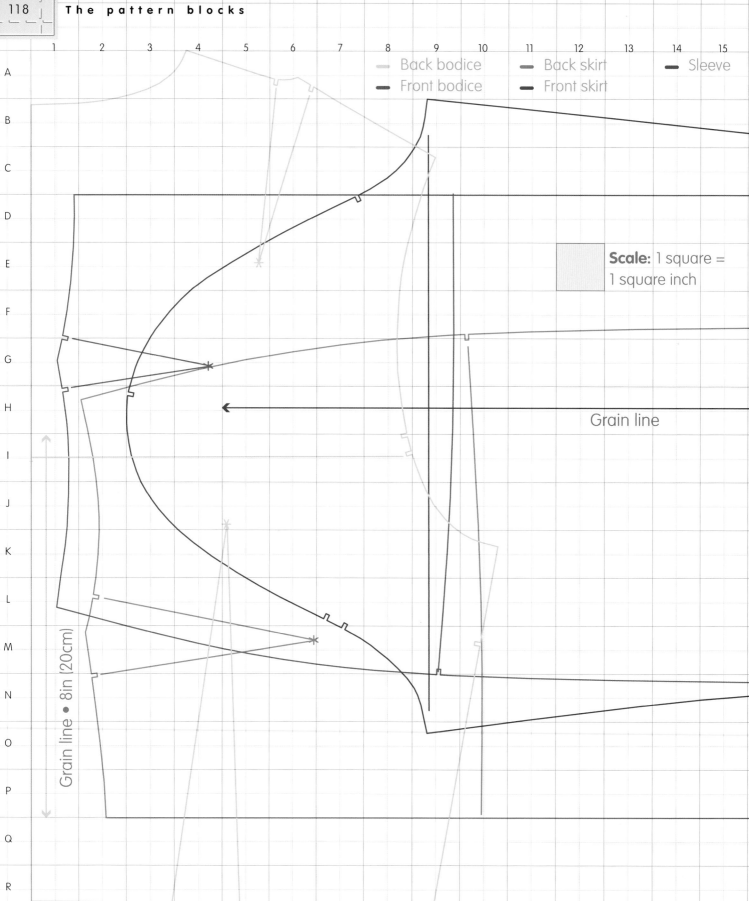

Back bodice   Back skirt   Sleeve
Front bodice   Front skirt

Scale: 1 square =
1 square inch

Grain line

Grain line • 8in (20cm)

US SIZE 12 pattern blocks

See page 66 for instructions on how to scale up the pattern blocks.

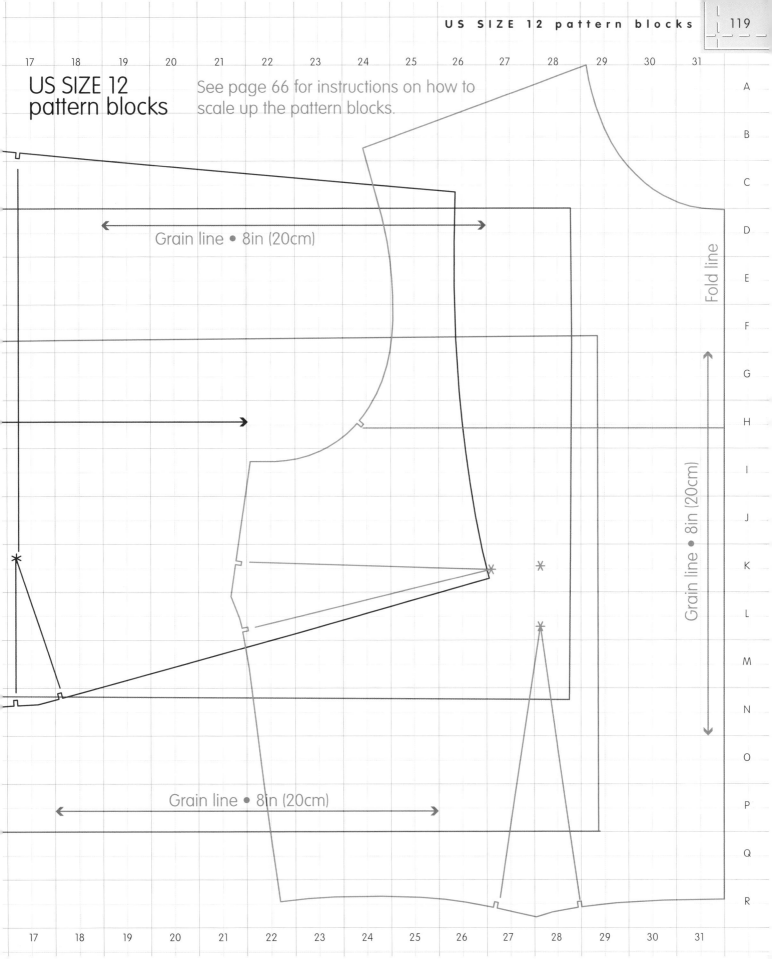

Grain line • 8in (20cm)

Fold line

Grain line • 8in (20cm)

Grain line • 8in (20cm)

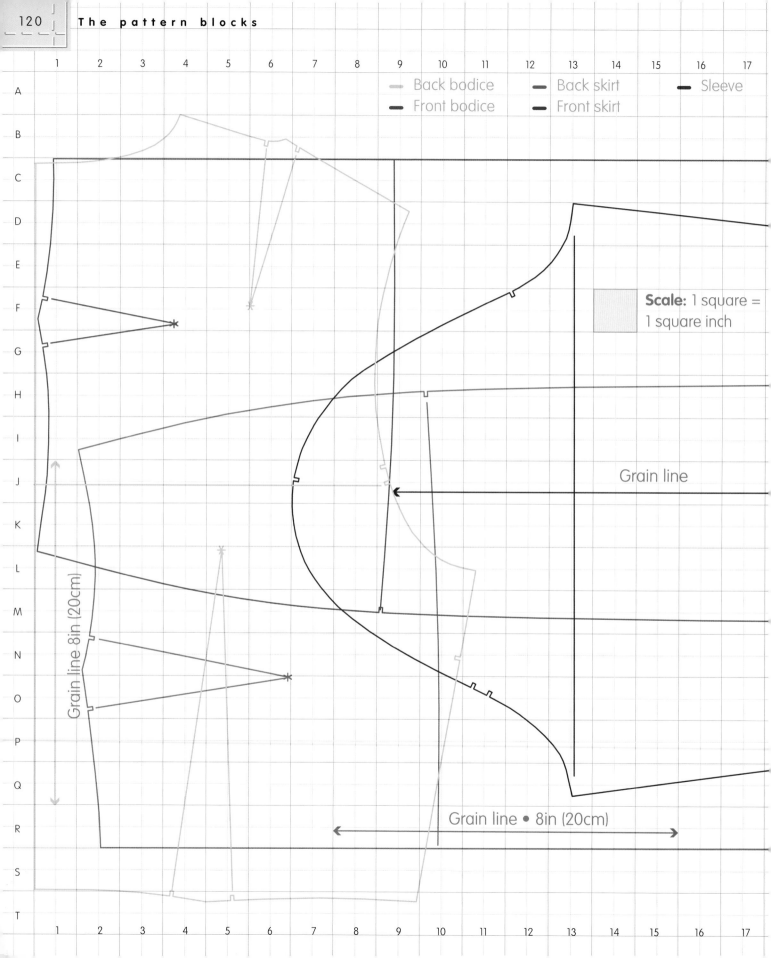

A B C D E F G H I J K L M N O P Q R S T

1 2 3 4 5 6 7 8 9 10 11 12 13 14 15 16 17

Back bodice　　Back skirt　　Sleeve

Front bodice　　Front skirt

Scale: 1 square = 1 square inch

Grain line

Grain line 8in (20cm)

Grain line • 8in (20cm)

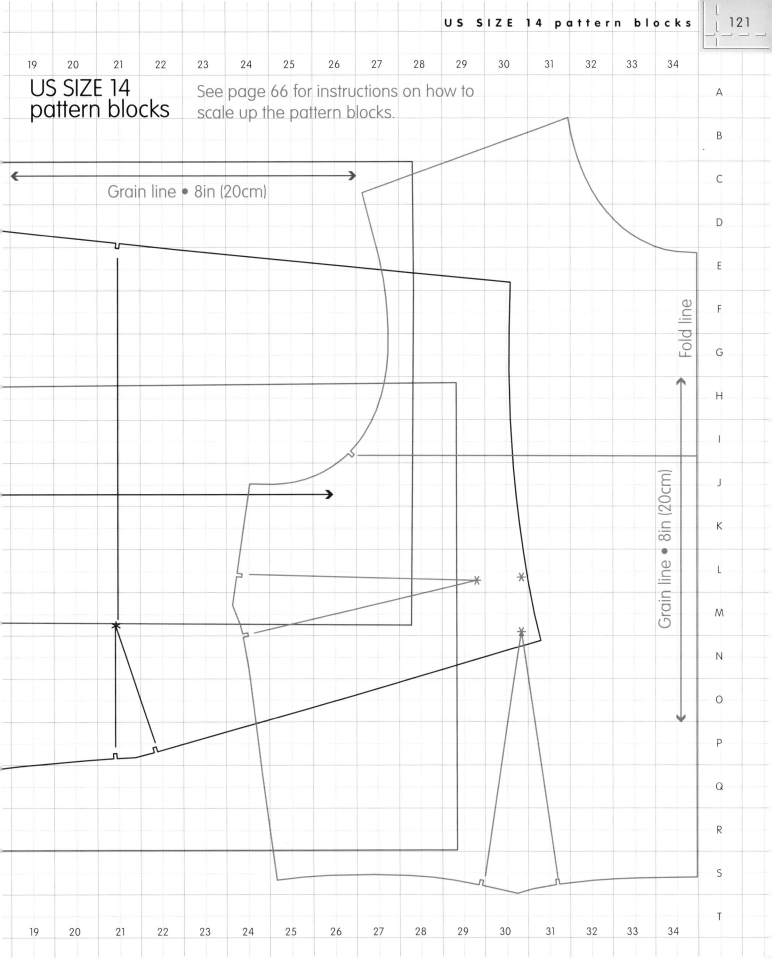

US SIZE 14
pattern blocks

See page 66 for instructions on how to scale up the pattern blocks.

Grain line • 8in (20cm)

Fold line

Grain line • 8in (20cm)

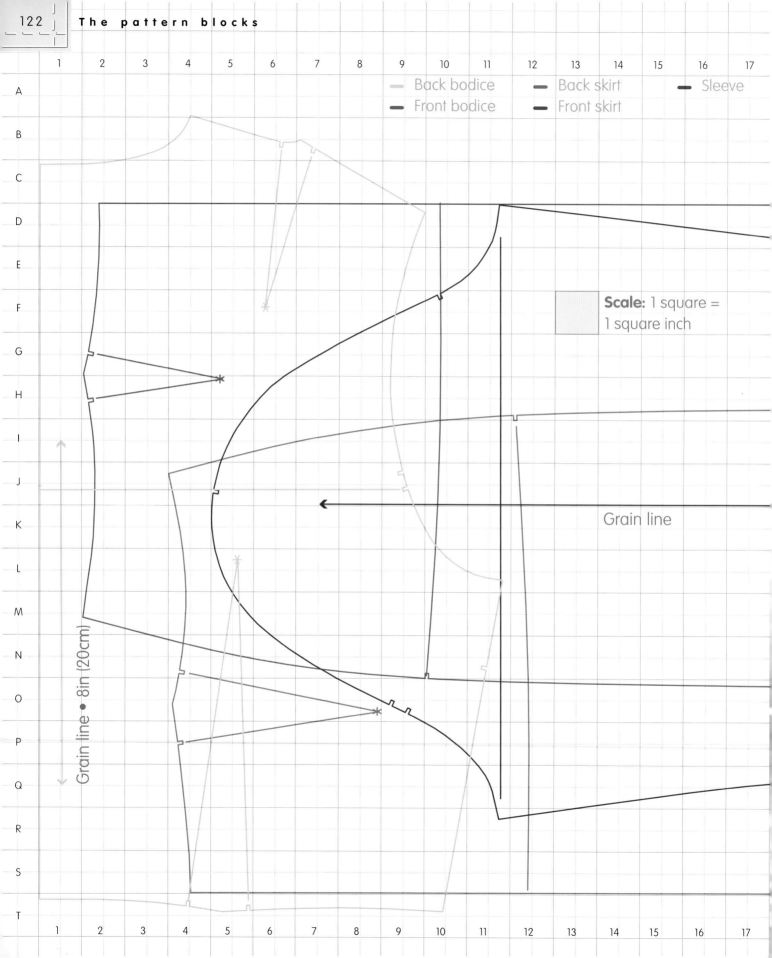

A   B   C   D   E   F   G   H   I   J   K   L   M   N   O   P   Q   R   S   T

Back bodice   Back skirt   Sleeve
Front bodice   Front skirt

Scale: 1 square = 1 square inch

Grain line

Grain line • 8in (20cm)

US SIZE 16 pattern blocks

See page 66 for instructions on how to scale up the pattern blocks.

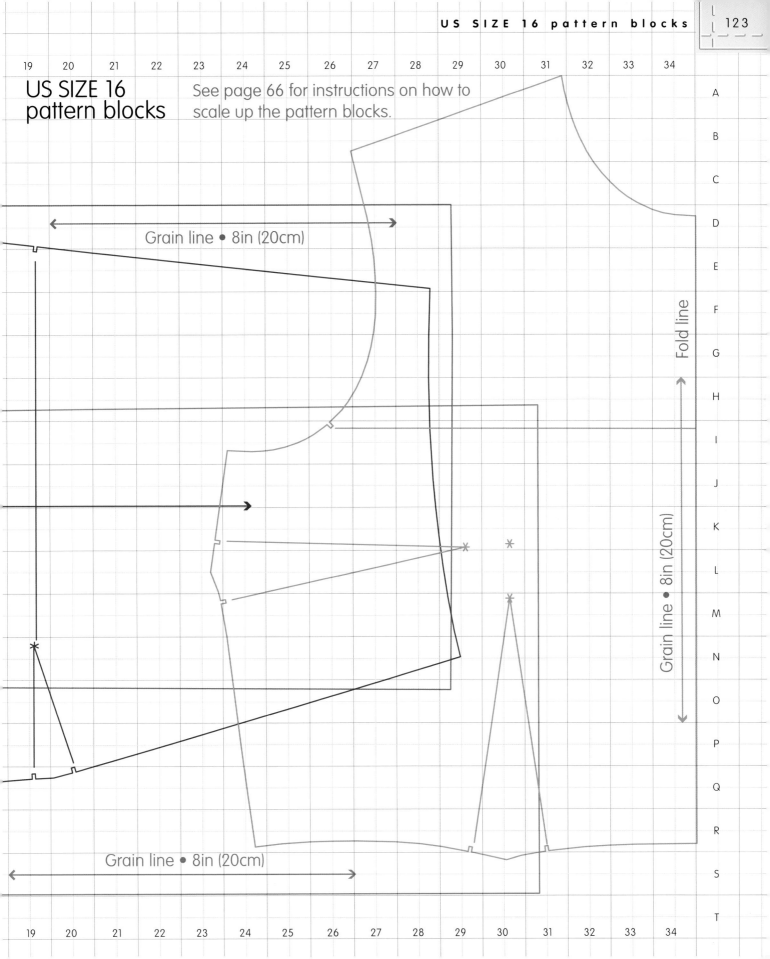

Grain line • 8in (20cm)

Fold line

Grain line • 8in (20cm)

Grain line • 8in (20cm)

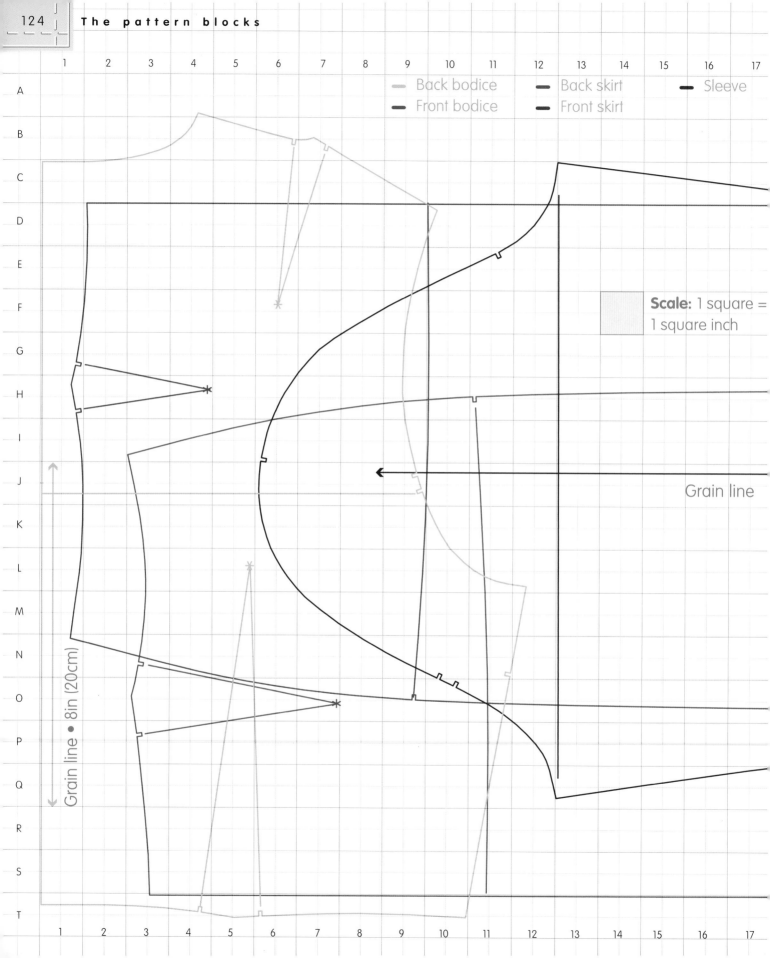

Back bodice — **Back skirt** — **Sleeve**

Front bodice — **Front skirt**

Scale: 1 square = 1 square inch

Grain line

Grain line • 8in (20cm)

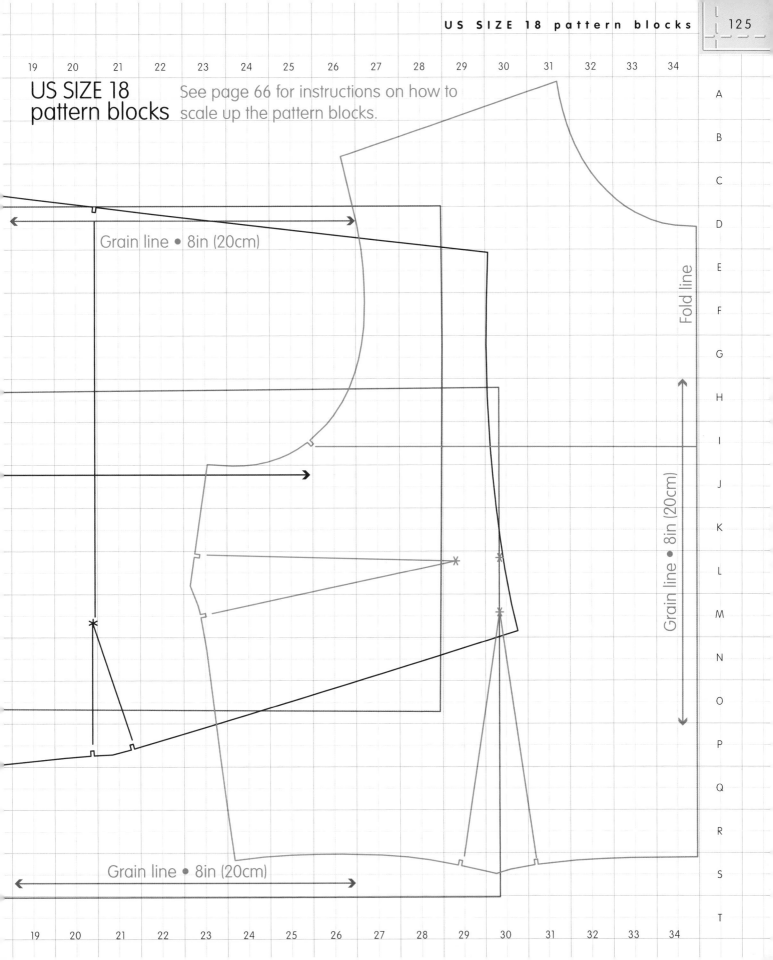

19 20 21 22 23 24 25 26 27 28 29 30 31 32 33 34

US SIZE 18 pattern blocks

See page 66 for instructions on how to scale up the pattern blocks.

A
B
C
D
E

Fold line

F
G
H
I
J
K
L
M
N
O
P
Q
R
S
T

Grain line • 8in (20cm)

Grain line • 8in (20cm)

Grain line • 8in (20cm)

19 20 21 22 23 24 25 26 27 28 29 30 31 32 33 34

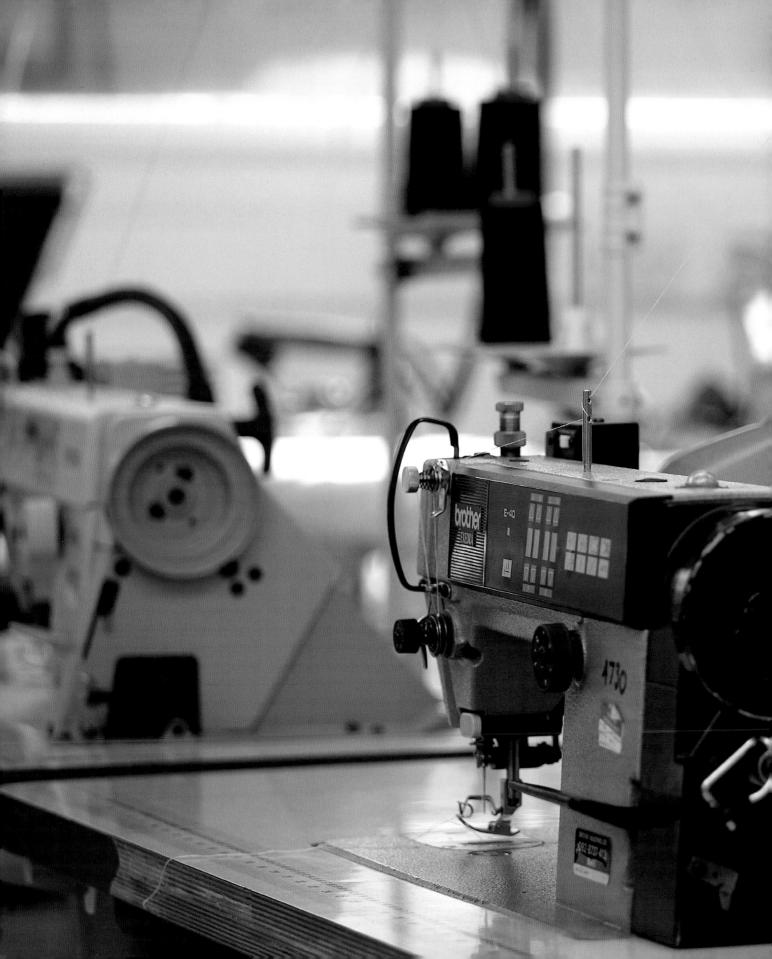

Core sewing techniques

This clear, step-by-step guide to core sewing techniques provides all the sewing knowledge you will need to create your own garments using the basic pattern blocks, from the different types of hems to adding details like pockets and collars.

Core sewing techniques

Essential sewing skills.

In order to carry out the techniques demonstrated in this book, you will need to have mastered core sewing and dressmaking skills. The following pages are a refresher course in all the techniques you will need to know.

French seam

A French seam encloses the raw edges, making additional finishing unnecessary. It looks flat like a plain seam from the front but appears like a tuck on the reverse.

 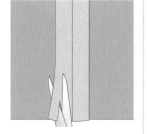

1 Place the wrong sides of the fabric together, with the edges matching. Sew with a straight stitch ¼in (6mm) from the edge.

2 Press the seam open and trim the raw edges to approximately half.

3 Fold the seam the opposite way, so that the right sides are now facing and the seam is pressed out to the edge.

4 Complete the seam with a final row of stitching ¼in (6mm) from the edge. This will enclose all the raw edges.

Plain seam

This is the simplest method of joining two pieces of fabric. Use it for straight or curved seams and all materials.

  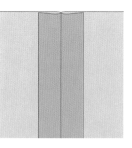

1 Place the right sides together, matching the raw edges, and pin along the sewing line.

2 Use a straight stitch and sew along the sewing line, removing the pins in the process.

3 Press the seam open or to one side and neaten using a seam finish.

Zigzag finish

This is a form of overcasting using a machine stitch. Use a zigzag stitch or a preprogrammed overcasting stitch to finish the raw edges.

 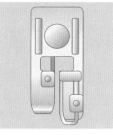 

1 Construct a plain seam. This is normally made with a ⅝in (1.5 cm) seam allowance.

2 Choose a zigzag stitch, or, if sewing a built-in overcasting machine stitch, use an overcasting foot.

3 Sew the stitch along the edge of the seam allowance with the "bar" of the overcasting foot right on the edge.

Serging

Serging is a good way to finish raw edges, since the stitches are formed over a newly trimmed edge to give a neat finish. A purpose-made machine is needed.

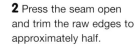 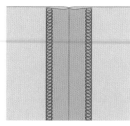 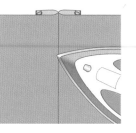

1 Make a seam with right sides together and sew a line of stitches ⅝in (1.5 cm) from the edge.

2 Thread the serger with three threads and skim each of the raw edges of the seam to finish.

3 Iron lightly over the right side to press.

Flat-fell seam

A flat-fell seam is popular for jeans and for reversible garments since it forms a strong and neat join; all the raw edges are tucked away and enclosed by a second line of stitching.

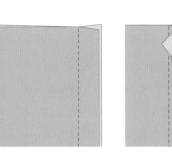

1 Place the wrong sides of the fabric together and sew a line of straight stitching ⅝in (1.5cm) from the edge.

2 Press the raw edges to one side and trim the underlayer to ⅛in (3mm).

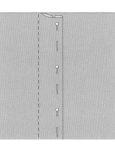

3 Fold the upper seam allowance under and place over the trimmed allowance. Pin all layers of fabric together.

4 Edge stitch the fold, sewing through all layers of fabric.

Bias binding

A bias binding gives a neat and strong finish to an edge. The bias nature of the tape allows it to curve over a shaped edge without wrinkling. Use it on seams and hems, and as a decorative finish.

1 Fold ready-made double-fold bias-binding tape in half to enclose the fabric's raw edges.

2 Place the folded tape over each raw edge and pin the layers together. Baste too, if preferred.

3 Sew through all layers with a straight stitch, keeping close to the binding edge.

4 Look at the reverse side to check that the tape is sewn down all along the edge.

Spaced tucks

Spaced tucks are folds of cloth sewn at regular intervals to add texture and interest to a garment. Sew them in groups and down the full length of the tuck, or leave them free at one end. Use vertically on a bodice or yoke, or horizontally around the bottom of a skirt.

1 Mark the position and size of the tucks onto the fabric's surface.

2 Fold the fabric along the lines with wrong sides together, and press with an iron.

3 With a straight stitch, sew parallel to each of the folded edges to form the tucks.

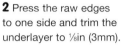

4 When all the tucks have been completed, press them all in the same direction.

Inverted pleats

Pleats can be stitched down or left to hang free from a seam or waistband, and either soft or pressed crisply. An inverted pleat consists of two folds that face each other.

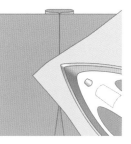

1 Mark the position and size of the pleat with tailor's tacks or chalk (on the wrong side of the fabric).

2 Fold the pleat through the center with the right sides of the cloth facing. Machine a straight stitch along the marked line.

3 Press the line of stitching and fold so the center crease lies directly below the seam. Baste within the seam allowance.

4 Press the inverted pleat, using a cloth to protect the surface, and continue with the next.

Elastic casing

The traditional way to elasticate an edge is to create a casing and then thread elastic through it. This allows the elastic to be adjusted easily—ideal for cuffs and waists.

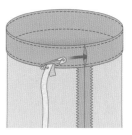

1 Sew the garment seams. It's easier to work with a continuous length—this will also give a neater finish.

2 Press the edge of the fabric under ¼in. (6mm) to the wrong side. Press again, the width of the elastic plus ⅛in (3mm). Pin in place.

3 With a straight stitch, sew the folded edge of the casing down. Sew over the first four stitches with the last four to secure the threads. Repeat around the top edge.

4 Remove the stitches from the seam and thread elastic through the casing. Adjust the length and secure ends of the elastic and seam.

Pants zipper

A pants, or fly-front zipper, completely hides the teeth and can be used for skirts and shorts as well as pants. For men, the zipper is inserted with the left side over the right, and for women the right is placed over the left.

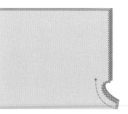

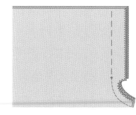

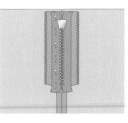

1 Machine stitch the seam from the base of the zipper to the crotch.

2 Machine baste the opening where the zipper will be inserted, using the longest straight stitch, and then finger press open.

3 With the right side of the pants facedown on your work surface, place the zipper facedown and centered over the basted seam. Pin the left side of the zipper tape to the seam allowance.

Centered zipper

This method places the zipper teeth in the middle of a seam. It's an easy technique ideal for beginners.

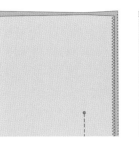

1 Make a plain seam ⅝–1 in (1.5–2.5cm) where the zipper is to be placed, leaving the zipper length unstitched.

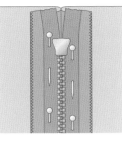

2 With the longest straight stitch, complete the seam. Don't finish the thread ends—these are temporary.

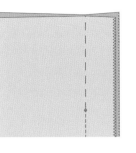

3 Press the seam open and with the wrong side facing up, place the zipper facedown with the teeth over the seam. Pin both sides.

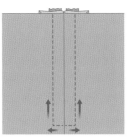

4 Baste the zipper in place and topstitch from the right side of the garment. Start from the bottom and sew to the top each time. Remove the temporary stitches.

Easing

Easing is achieved in the same way as gathering, but the fabric takes on a shape without visible tucks. Use it to set in a sleeve or fit a skirt into a waistband.

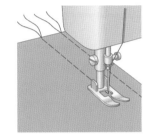

1 Set the sewing machine to the longest straight stitch.

2 Sew two parallel lines on either side of the stitching line ⅛in (3mm) apart.

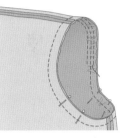

3 Pull up the fabric along the gathering threads to ease it to the size of the adjoining fabric. Distribute the fullness evenly. There shouldn't be any tucks or gathers.

4 Pin and sew to the armhole or waistband as required, and then remove the gathering stitches.

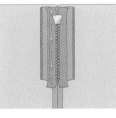

4 Attach a zipper foot to the machine and sew through the tape and the seam allowance, approximately ¼in (6 mm) from the edge of the tape.

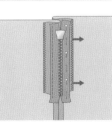

5 Pull the zipper to the right and pin the zipper tape to the right edge through all layers. Turn the work over and re-pin neatly, flattening any wrinkles.

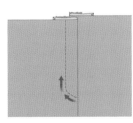

6 Mark a guideline with chalk or a temporary marker, and topstitch from the base of the zipper to the waist line to secure it in place. Remove all basting stitches and test the zipper.

7 Cut a piece of fabric approximately 4in (10 cm) wide and longer than the zipper. Fold with right sides of the fabric together, and sew. Trim the seam allowances and turn through to create a guard. Press flat.

8 Stitch the guard in place on the inside, attaching it to the seam allowance so that the stitches will not be seen on the outside.

Fusible interfacings

This new generation of interfacings are either woven or bonded fabric with a heat-fusible glue on one side. They do away with the need for hand stitching and allow for a much faster construction of tailored garments.

Fusing the interfacing to the underside of the fabric

1 Cut the pieces out as necessary and place the fabric facedown on the ironing board.

2 Trim the interfacing to ensure it is ¹⁄₁₆in. (1 mm) smaller than the garment piece so that the glue will not stick to the ironing board. Place the interfacing glue-side-down on the fabric.

3 With a steam iron, hover over the interfacing and pump steam over the pieces.

4 Slowly press the interfacing to the fabric until the pieces are fused together.

Traditional waistband

A waistband is added to a skirt or pants to finish the edge, and it may open at the front, side, or center back. This type is suitable for all styles of garments that incorporate gathers, darts, tucks, or pleats. An interfacing is needed to add body to the band and to help it stay in place. Soft perforated interfacings, as well as straight or curved stiff bands, are available in various widths. These can be fused to the wrong side of the fabric or sewn in place.

1 Cut the waistband to the correct length and width, along with added seam allowances. Mount the interfacing to the wrong side of the fabric.

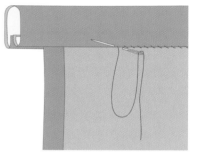

2 Place the raw edge of the waistband to the waist line edge of the garment, with right sides together. Pin and then machine sew with a straight stitch.

3 Fold the waistband lengthwise and press it up and over the waist to conceal the raw edges. Fold the opposite edge under and pin in place, leaving one end extended ¼in (3cm) for the fasteners. Sew down by machine stitching in the ditch from the outside, or by hand, hemming on the inside.

4 Finish the ends of the waistband by folding one edge in and slip stitching. On the opposite, longer end, tuck the raw edges in and slip stitch to finish. Sew hooks and eyes, or a button and buttonhole in place to finish.

Alternative finish

Neaten the raw edge of the waistband with a serger stitch or a zigzag stitch and lay flat on the inside without folding under. Stitch in the ditch to secure.

Double-folded hem

A double-folded hem is folded twice to conceal the raw edges within. It may be wide or narrow, and finished by hand or with machine topstitching. Use it on woven and knitted fabrics to provide a neatly finished edge on shirts, blouses, T-shirts, and pants.

1 Fold the raw edge to the hem level around the circumference of the hem.

2 Fold up again to conceal the raw edge at hem level and pin to hold it in place.

3 Neatly sew the hem by hand or with machine topstitching.

Hand-finished hem

A hand-sewn hem is the best option for skirts and pants where stitches should not be visible on the right side. Hem stitch, slip stitch, herringbone stitch, and lockstitch are all useful, and your choice of one of them will depend on the type and weight of your fabric as well as your personal preference. A hand-stitched hem isn't as strong as a machined one, but the stitches will be invisible.

1 Prepare the hem by folding up on the hem line and tucking the seam allowance under.

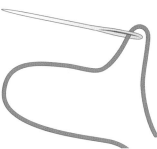

2 Cut a short length of silk thread in a matching shade and thread onto a short, fine needle.

3 Complete the hem with your preferred stitch:

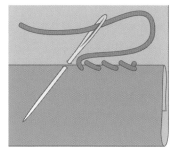

Hem stitch
Use hem stitch where a strong finish is required, such as on medium- to heavy-weight fabric.

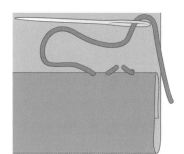

Slip stitch
This method is less visible than hem stitch, so it is suitable for fine material. For a good result, keep the stitches well spaced, yet even. Always use a thread in a closely matching shade.

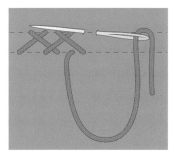

Herringbone stitch
This stitch is suitable for both medium- and heavy-weight stretch fabrics since the stitches "give" if the hem is pulled.

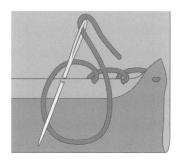

Lockstitch
Thread loops around each stitch in a lockstitched hem. This means that if the thread breaks, the hem will not unravel fully. Keep the stitches well spaced and even. This is a suitable method for all fabric weights.

Eased-in sleeve

A sleeve that is eased into the shoulder area produces a smooth finish with no tucks or crinkles. The sleeve itself may be short or long, slim-fitting or flared, but should lie in a simple, flat line where it is attached to the shoulder.

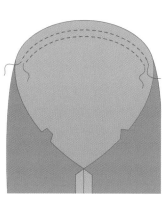
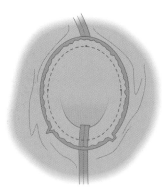

Preparation

Complete the shoulder and side seam of the bodice and the sleeve seams. It may even be best to complete the sleeve hem or cuff before sewing the sleeve into the armhole.

1 Set the sewing machine to the longest straight stitch and sew two parallel lines along the edge of the sleeve cap between the pattern-marking dots, on either side of the seam line (or inside the seam line in the case of delicate fabrics).

2 Ease up the gathers and place the sleeve in the armhole with right sides together and raw edges matching. Working from inside the sleeve, match up the pattern notches, dots, and seams. Pin along the seam line, distributing the tiny gathers evenly until they disappear.

3 While it is in the pinned state, turn it through and check the finished look. Adjust the eased fabric, if necessary, and then turn back again and sew with a standard-length straight stitch. Check the finished sleeve seam, and neaten the raw edges on the inside with a three-thread serger stitch or use a sewing machine zigzag or other suitable stitch. Trim the excess fabric away.

Gathered sleeve head

On a gathered sleeve head, clearly defined tucks create fullness along the shoulder seam. Fashion trends change frequently, but a puffed sleeve is always popular for little girls' dresses. This technique is easier than an eased-in sleeve, but it's important to arrange the gathers evenly.

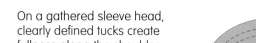
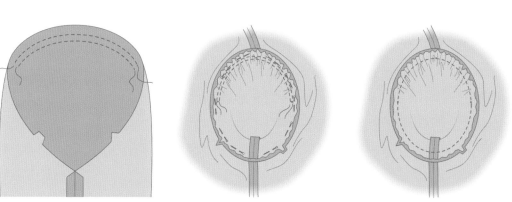

Preparation

Complete the shoulder and side seams of the garment as well as the sleeve seam, hem, and the cuff if there is one, before inserting the sleeve. (It's easier to finish a cuff when handling it as a single sleeve than when it's attached to an entire garment.)

1 Set the sewing machine to the longest straight stitch and sew two parallel lines between the pattern-marked dots, on either side of the cap seam line (or just within the seam allowance if working with delicate fabrics).

2 Place the sleeve in the armhole and match up the pattern dots and notches. Pull up the gathers and arrange them across the top of the sleeve. Pin on the seam line from the inside. Baste the seam to hold the gathers evenly in place.

3 Turn through and check to see that the gathers are sitting neatly; then machine along the seam line. Remove the temporary gathering stitches and neaten the raw edges. Press the seam allowance toward the sleeve.

Shirt cuff

A traditional tailored shirt cuff is stiffened with collar and cuff canvas. This gives a crisp, neat appearance. Stiff, fusible interfacings can be used, but the technique suggested below combines a more rigid canvas with a lightweight fusible interfacing.

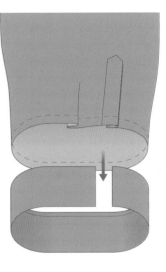

Preparation

For each cuff, cut out two in the shirt fabric, one in lightweight fusible interfacing and one in the cuff canvas.

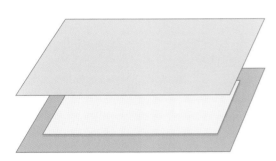

1 With a pencil and ruler, mark the seam allowances on the cuff-canvas pieces ⅝in (1.5cm) from the edges. Cut off the seam allowances, including the pencil line.

2 Place the shirt cuff on the ironing board with the wrong side facing up. Position the canvas in the center of the cuff. Place the fusible interfacing (glue side down) on top, sandwiching the canvas in the middle. Iron the layers carefully and fuse the pieces together.

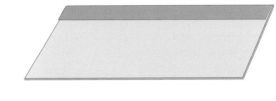

3 Press the seam allowance of the top edge of the cuff to the wrong side over the canvas. This gives a sharp edge.

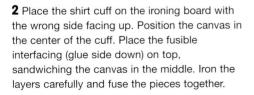

4 Place the cuff to its facing with right sides together. Sew along the stitching line, around the outside, adjacent to the canvas but not through it.

5 Layer the seam allowances and fold in the corners before turning through.

6 Fold the seam edge of the cuff facing in, and then slip the sleeve into the cuff and pin in place. Working from the right side, edge stitch and topstitch the cuff to the sleeve.

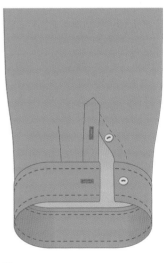

7 Add buttonholes and sew buttons in position.

Shoulder pad

Shoulder pads can make or break a garment. Our less-than-perfect bodies don't always provide the best shape to carry a great jacket or coat! At times in fashion history, shoulder pads have been oversized, but without them a garment lacks support. The paddings and canvases used on the inside to construct a jacket or coat work with shoulder pads to create an internal hanger.

 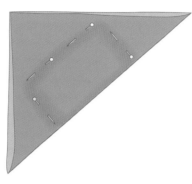

1 Place a square of gauze on the work surface and cover it with a square of low-loft batting or volume fleece. Position a shoulder pad diagonally across the center.

2 Wrap up the shoulder pad and pin the layers together around the outer edge.

3 Determine the exact shape and size required and zigzag around the edge. Cut away the excess fabric.

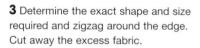
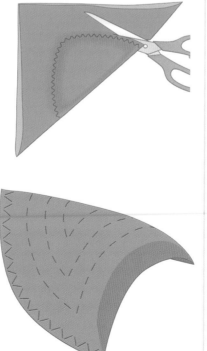

4 Hand stitch and quilt the shoulder pad, starting from the outside and working toward the center. Manipulate the pad into shape and sew in place in the garment.

Yoke

A yoke covers an area of the upper back and shoulders and includes an outer layer and under layer or facing. It conceals raw edges and provides both additional weight and support.

Preparation
The fronts and back should be ready with gathers, pleats, or other finishes completed.

1 Place the right side of the outer yoke to the right side of the back. Match balance points and pin together.

2 Place the right side of the under yoke to the wrong side of the back, sandwiching the back between the two yoke pieces. Re-pin and sew on the stitching line.

4 Place the front of the outer yoke to the front pieces with right sides together. Match all of the notches, and then pin and sew together.

5 Fold under the seam allowances on the front edges of the facing and match with the front seams of the yoke.

Shirt collar

A shirt collar is an extension of the collar stand, but in this case, the "stand" (see page 100) sits on the neckline edge and the "fall" is the upper part of the collar that drops down to cover the stand. Tailored shirt collars are normally firm and can be worn either with the stand buttoned up close to the neck and worn with a necktie—or open, without a necktie. The firmness of the interfacing will determine how tailored or casual the collar will be. The collar fall can be buttoned down, or not, and points can be sharply angled or even rounded to a curve.

Preparation

Complete the neck edge so it is ready to attach the collar.

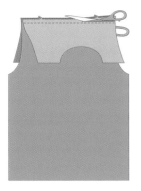

3 Trim and layer the seam allowances.

6 Hand sew or top- and edge-stitch the layers together to complete the yoke.

1 For the collar, draw the seam allowance on the outer edges of the stiff collar interfacing. Trim this away, including the pencil line.

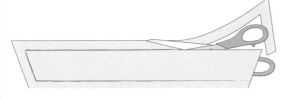

2 Center the stiff interfacing on the wrong side of the upper collar and place the lightweight fusible interfacing on top. Fuse in place, sandwiching the stiff interfacing between the upper collar and the fusible layer.

3 Place the upper and lower collar (the collar facing) together with right sides together. Mark the collar points with a fade-away marker or tailor's tack, and sew along the seam line. Trim the seam allowances; turn through and press flat. Finish with edge stitching.

4 Prepare the stiff interfacing for the collar stand in the same way as above, fusing it to the side that will lie next to the neck.

5 Sandwich the collar between the collar stand pieces, matching any pattern-marked notches and dots. Sew these together, layer the seam allowances inside, turn to the right side, and iron to create a crisp finish.

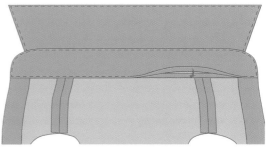

6 Join the outside of the collar stand to the right side of the neck edge and sew together. (Snip into the seam allowance of the neck edge to allow easy matching if necessary.)

7 Tuck up the seam allowance on the inside of the collar stand and pin in place. Edge stitch through all layers.

Patch pocket

A patch pocket is one of the simplest pockets to create. It is placed to the right side of the fabric and sewn in place with topstitching. It may be lined or left unlined with the seam allowances just pressed under before attaching it.

Preparation

Iron a piece of lightweight fusible interfacing to the wrong side of the fabric to strengthen the pocket.

Without a lining

1 Make a card template of the finished pocket minus the seam allowances.

2 Neaten the upper edge of the pocket and fold the top edge to the right side of the fabric. Stitch on the seam line.

3 Turn the top edge through and slip the card template inside. Place the pocket facedown on the ironing board with the template inside, and press the edges up and over the card to set the shape of the pocket. Baste to hold the shape, and machine sew the upper edge.

4 Place the pocket on the garment and edge- and top-stitch in place. Finish with bar tacks at the top corners to give additional strength.

With a lining

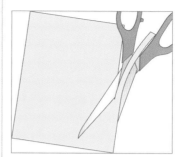

1 Trim 1/16in (2mm) from the edge of the lining.

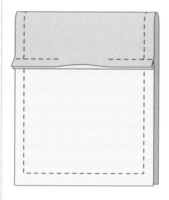

3 With right sides together and edges matching, pin around the outside edge, and then machine the two layers together.

5 Close the opening with hand-sewn slip stitches, or use topstitching from the right side as a decorative effect. (This will close the hole in the seam at the same time.)

2 Sew the lining to the pocket front, right sides together, leaving a gap of approximately 1½in. (4cm) in the middle of the seam. Press the raw edges toward the lining.

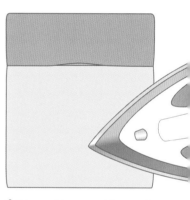

4 Trim and layer, and then pull through the hole left between the lining and pocket, and press flat.

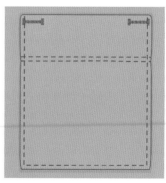

6 Place the pocket in position and edge stitch to secure in position. Add topstitching, too, if desired, and finish with bar tacks to strengthen the top corners.

Lining a dress

There are so many dress styles that each design will dictate details on how the lining is to be cut and attached. On the whole, however, if the dress has a waist, the bodice and skirt linings will be cut separately and joined there.

Preparation
Construct the bodice and skirt parts of the dress.

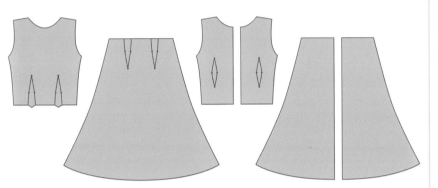

1 Cut out the lining pieces in suitable fabric. Use the dress pattern pieces if lining pattern pieces are not included.

 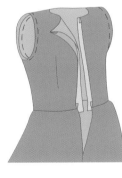 

2 Construct the skirt and baste to the seam allowance at the waist of the bodice. Stitch in place, sewing just inside the seam line.

3 Depending on the style of neckline, the lining may be machine sewed directly to the neck or to a facing. When the neckline is complete, attach the bodice lining to the dress at the armhole by basting within the seam allowance.

4 Tuck under the seam allowance at the waist and pin over the skirt and lining. Slip stitch together. Tuck the seam allowance under at the zipper and slip stitch. To finish, sew in sleeves, lined or otherwise, and finish the seam edges.

Lining a skirt

Lining a skirt will add body, make it more comfortable, and prolong its life. Any skirt, whether straight, flared, gathered, or pleated, can be lined. As a general rule, the skirt pattern is cut out and made up in lining fabric, then attached at the waist; no separate pattern is needed.

Straight or A-line skirt

1 Cut out the skirt pieces in lining fabric and sew the skirt lining together, right sides facing. Leave a gap at the zipper position and at the back vent if there is one. Mark the dart positions but leave them unsewn.

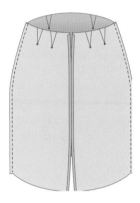

2 Drop the lining into the skirt with wrong sides together. Pin at the waist and tuck in the darts, and then baste.

3 Tuck the seam allowance under at the zipper and slip stitch in place. Add the waistband, sewing the skirt and lining as one, and neaten the hem of the lining. Leave the lining back vent open; just neaten the raw edges.

Glossary

Balance points
Balance points are marks that refer to all notches and dots that help to align fabric pieces when constructing a garment.

Basic blocks
The basic flat components of skirt, bodice, and sleeve for example, from which you create a fully detailed sewing pattern.

Basting
Temporary stitching by hand or machine. Also known as tacking.

Batting
Used in quilting, this material is a thick, soft layer of insulation that sits between the surface fabric and the backing fabric. It is also known as wadding.

Bias/cross grain of fabric
The diagonal direction of fabric between the warp and the weft threads.

Cutting layout
The manufacturer's guide to laying pattern pieces on fabric in the most economical way and keeping pieces "on grain" or on fold lines, and so on. A number of layouts are provided for different fabric widths and pattern sizes.

Dart
A dart is a wedge of fabric that is pinched out of a garment to allow shaping or to remove excess fabric.

Dress form
A mannequin used to assist in the making up of garments.

Ease
Ease refers to the amount of space built into a sewing pattern—in addition to body measurements—to allow movement and to achieve the required garment silhouette.

Flat pattern cutting
A two-dimensional approach to creating and developing paper sewing patterns based on basic blocks.

Fold line
Used to describe the position of pattern pieces to be placed on folded fabric. The fabric is folded, right sides together, usually lengthwise so that the selvages are together. A directional arrow on the pattern tissue indicates how to place the piece on the folded fabric.

Grain line
The fabric grain is the direction of the woven fibers. Straight or lengthwise grain runs along the warp thread, parallel to the selvages. Crosswise grain runs

along the weft, perpendicular to straight grain. Most dressmaking pattern pieces are cut on the lengthwise grain, which has minimal stretch.

Hand/handle
The term used to describe how a fabric feels, drapes, folds, pleats, etc. For example, this may be crisp, soft, heavy, or stiff.

Interfacing
A stabilizing fabric used on the wrong side of the fabric to support a piece of a garment, for example a collar or behind a pocket.

Lining
A separate fabric sewn onto the inside of a garment to conceal all raw edges and help it to hang well.

Mercerized cotton
A treatment applied to give strength and luster.

Nap
The shading that occurs on piled fabrics. Pile is the term for the raised fibers on fabrics such as velvets and furs. A "with nap" cutting layout is used for fabrics with a pile, one-way shading, or design. Patterns are placed so that the pile will run in the same direction on all corresponding pieces.

Natural fiber
Fiber from a non-synthetic source, e.g., cotton or flax plant, silk moth, or wool.

Notches
Triangular markings on the pattern tissue used to match two corresponding pieces. They can be single, double, or triple, and have the same combination of notches on pieces to be joined.

Placement lines
The lines printed on pattern tissue, indicating where design details, such as pockets, welt flaps, and front plackets, should be placed.

Princess line
A dress with curved seaming running from the shoulder or the armhole to the hem on the front and back, giving six panels (not including the center back seam).

Seam allowance
The area between the sewing line and the edge of the cloth normally $5/8$in (1.5cm), but 1in (2.5cm) in couture sewing.

Selvage
The side edges of fabric. These are often bound more tightly than the fabric weave.

Serger
A machine designed to sew and finish edges in one step, although it can produce many other effects too. Also known as an overlocker.

Silk
There are many types of silk fabric, each with a slightly different finish. Fabric names include charmeuse, chiffon, crepe de Chine, dupion, gazar, georgette, noil, organza, raw, sandwashed, shantung, Thai, and tussah.

Slash and spread
A method for adding fullness to a pattern, whereby the pattern piece is slashed apart, spread out, and re-drawn with added volume.

"Stitch in the Ditch" (sink stitch)
Used to describe where pieces are held together by stitching on the right side of a previously made seam, e.g., on a waistband.

Synthetic fiber
Fibers from a non-natural source, e.g., nylon, polyester, and acrylic.

Tailor's tacks
A temporary stitch used to mark the placement of details, such as pockets on a piece of fabric to be made up into a garment.

Toile
An early prototype of a garment made in inexpensive fabric.

Torso block
A torso block is a bodice that extends down to the hip line.

Index

Credits

Quarto would like to thank and
acknowledge the following for their
contribution to this book:

The McCall Pattern Company
Butterick, McCall, Vogue Patterns
120 Broadway
34th Floor
New York
NY 10271-3499, USA
www.mccallpattern.com
www.butterick.com
www.voguepatterns.com

Verlag Aenne Burda GmbH & Co. KG
Fashion Factory
Am Kestendamm 2
D - 77652 Offenburg
www.burdastyle.com